MY LIFE WITH TOYOTA
SHOTARO KAMIYA

Published by

TOYOTA MOTOR SALES COMPANY, LTD.

Translated by Thomas I. Elliott
Editing/compilation by GENDAI Advanced Studies Research Organization
Designed by Akira Mabuchi
Printed in Japan by Dai Nippon Printing Co.
First printing October 1976

Shotaro Kamiya
Chairman
Toyota Motor Sales Co., Ltd.

MY LIFE WITH TOYOTA

CONTENTS

FOREWORD

Over the years our Japanese affiliate Esso Sekiyu has had a long-lasting and cordial business relationship with Toyota Motor Sales Company. It is under these circumstances that I first met Mr. Shotaro Kamiya and on subsequent occasions I had several opportunities to visit with him during my travels to Japan.

These get-togethers — that I might add were all too infrequent — provided me with a chance to exchange views on international business which I found particularly helpful in gaining a better

perspective of the various challenges that Exxon faces in its everyday business. These same meetings also convinced me that Mr. Kamiya is one of the truly great businessmen in Japan. It is due largely to his leadership and management know-how that Toyota has achieved unparalleled success in the international marketplace both in terms of sales and profit growth. Equally important in my view is the high esprit de corps that he has established throughout the Toyota sales and dealer organizations. This team spirit, coupled with Mr. Kamiya's guiding principle that "the policies of a corporation must conform not only to the interests of Japan, but also to the needs of every society, however great or small," is bound to assure Toyota's success for many years to come.

My Life With Toyota provides the reader with an insight into the man — Shotaro Kamiya — and how he has been inspired over the years by the Shogun Ieyasu Tokugawa's statement "to shoulder a heavy burden down a long road — such is life."

J.K. Jamieson -
Chairman of the Board
(Retired)
Exxon Corporation

INTRODUCTION

Shotaro Kamiya and I first met in 1930, the year that I joined General Motors-Japan. I was assigned to the Sales and Publicity Department, and he was Department Manager there. That assignment was thus my introduction to the automobile industry and the start of a working relationship with Shotaro Kamiya that has spanned almost half a century.

In reflecting back over the years I realize now how very fortunate I was to have had Kamiya as my supervisor in 1930. By having met him in that way almost fifty years ago I was able later to participate in the great drama of the birth, growth and maturation of Japan's automobile industry.

I developed an unshakably strong trust of and admiration for Shotaro Kamiya during the first five years that I worked under him, and in 1935 when he confided in me his decision to leave General Motors and join Toyoda Automatic Loom Works, which was then working to produce a wholly domestic-made passenger car, I told him that I would go with him.

However, after Kamiya left GM and joined Toyoda he learned more about Toyoda's plans and found that the over-all circumstances, including his own salary, were much worse than he had imagined. He wrote and suggested that I rethink my decision to join him.

But, like Kamiya, my decision to work in Toyoda was not basically a financial decision. I trusted Kamiya and wanted to work with him, and I was excited by the idea of helping to produce a domestic-made passenger car. I wrote him and said I saw no need to rethink my decision.

I was in Osaka the morning that his reply telegram came to me from Nagoya. All the telegram said was "Come — but be prepared for the worst."

His few words told me there were serious difficulties that would have to be overcome before Toyoda could produce domestic-made vehicles. But his words also had a highly stirring ring which strengthened my resolve to join him.

My decision to go to Nagoya thus started me down a path with Kamiya that has since been a lifetime of work in Toyota. The path was not always smooth, but I will leave Kamiya himself to tell that story in the following pages. One thing I do want to say, however, is that back in the 1930s, and even as recently as 1950, the year that Toyota Motor Sales Company was founded, no one — not Kamiya, not I, nor anyone else — could possibly have ever forecast either the present prosperity of Japan's automobile industry or Toyota's amazing success.

In 1950, for example, the combined production of passenger cars and trucks by the entire automobile industry in Japan was still only 32,500 vehicles, and Toyota's total production that year was only 11,700 vehicles. But twenty-five years later, in 1975, Japan had grown to become second only to the United States in the number of automobiles produced, and Toyota had grown to become number three among the world's automakers in annual production, with over two million vehicles produced that year. I am proud when I think about what those figures mean in terms of the industry as I knew it in the 1930s.

Japan's automobile industry has truly grown, especially in recent years. I think the industry was fortunate because external conditions existed that favored its growth, but I would also emphasize the important role played by policies that Shotaro Kamiya initiated. Many of his early policies contributed to popularizing the automobile in Japan even before motorization's rapid spread, and he was thus a leader in promoting the industry's growth. His policies helped to create an environment that fostered the introduction of a modernized marketing system and later made volume sales possible. His tremendous foresight and innovativeness were obvious in everything he did — for example, in his zealous development of export markets. I can state with conviction that his efforts were key to the over-all prosperity of Japan's automobile industry, and, by extension, to Toyota's amazing growth.

Because I have worked closely together with Shotaro Kamiya for almost fifty years, most of the story that he tells in *My Life With Toyota* fills me with nostalgia and moves me deeply. While this book is an autobiography, it can also be read as a history of the Japanese automobile industry and a history of Toyota.

Infused throughout this book is the spirit of Shotaro Kamiya's belief that one must consider the future carefully but must act with force and determination. This book gives the reader a glimpse into the life of a great man.

15

Seisi Kato
President
Toyota Motor Sales Co., Ltd.

MY LIFE WITH TOYOTA

Chapter One

Out into the World

I was born in Yokosuka, a small town in Aichi Prefecture, on July 9, 1898, and while still a child I was adopted by the Kamiya family in Gokiso, Showa Ward, Nagoya City. My foster father had his own flour and noodle-making business. As the only boy in the family I was raised with special care, and I remember being a favorite of my mother.

As a boy, I seem to have had a stubborn streak. Once I set my mind to doing something I stayed until I finished it, a trait that made me somewhat of a leader among boyhood friends.

My higher education was at the Nagoya Commercial High School, where most of the students were sons of merchants from Nagoya and its surrounding area. As the son of a local businessman it was taken for granted that I would study

All footnotes refer to information in the appendices prepared to help the reader appreciate Mr. Kamiya's story more fully.

there. I was in the school's debating and *kendo* (Japanese fencing) clubs. These activities helped me train myself mentally and physically, although I was neither an outstanding scholar nor an athlete. My school years passed by quite ordinarily, but while in school I acquired a wide interest in other countries that remained with me throughout my life. I acquired this interest from Mr. Yoshiki Ichimura, the Principal of the school. I remember that he emphasized the need for Japan to become a trading nation. In fact, a wooden plaque with large Chinese characters on it that read "The world is our market" hung at the entrance to the school's main building. Mr. Ichimura spoke of the day when Japan would be a leader in world trade, and always urged his students to turn their eyes outward. Because of his influence I began thinking seriously about other nations, and without being conscious of it I acquired a habit of viewing matters from an international perspective.

Toward the end of my senior year at the Nagoya Commercial High School, my faculty adviser suggested that I continue my studies at a military academy. Although I leaned toward going, my father opposed the idea because I was an only son. There was also talk at the time about having me study further at a commercial college, but family circumstances did not allow this either. In the end I decided to look for a job. Because of my interest in business and international affairs, Mitsui & Company was my first choice. I asked Mr. Ichimura for a personal recommendation and applied at Mitsui.

Mitsui & Co. is a well-known trading company today, and even in 1917 it was already one of Japan's top firms. When I applied for work the company was in the process of vigorously expanding by opening new branch and representative offices overseas. I had hopes of being hired because graduation from the Nagoya Commercial High School put me in a category that under new company policy would let me be employed without an examination. Previously, selection of graduates from schools

19

other than Imperial universities and certain other schools was made on the basis of tough competitive examinations, but as part of the company's expansion plans it was decided that students from prefectural commercial schools with a good academic background and outstanding character could be employed after careful review but without an examination.

That was 1917, just when the United States had declared war on Germany and World War I was reaching its peak. Mitsui would be my first job, and I remember my enthusiasm for wanting to learn the trading business.

When I joined Mitsui I was asked by the personnel manager what department I wanted to work in. Almost without hesitating I replied that I wanted to work overseas, in New York if possible. I did not really expect an overseas post, since I was a new employee fresh from the provinces, but the words on the wooden plaque at the entrance to the Nagoya Commercial High School, "The world is our market," were still vividly in my mind and prompted me to say what I felt.

My hope for work overseas was realized earlier than I expected. In the spring of 1918, about one year after joining Mitsui, I was surprised one day to be informed that I was to be transferred to the Seattle Office, an office opened in 1916 as part of Mitsui's overseas expansion plan. It was a small office, nowhere near the size of the New York or London offices, but its volume of trading, especially in lumber, was expanding quickly. I was to be sent there to bolster the staff.

Although I had orginally asked to work in New York, I did not really expect to be sent there, and I was happy with the chance to go anywhere overseas, especially to the United States. While preparing for my voyage to Seattle, my excitement in thinking about work in a strange country completely suppressed any feeling of loneliness I might have had about leaving home. I was determined, and my determination was helping me through difficulties.

See p. 100, Col. A, "Sino-Japanese and Russo-Japanese Wars, and Japan's Industrialization."

The manager of the Seattle Office was Reisuke Ishida, a man who in later years became president of Mitsui & Company, then president of the Japan Trade Commission and then director of the Japanese National Railways. When I met him in 1918 he was thirty-two years old, one of Mitsui's elite young hopefuls and an excellent manager with a keen mind for anticipating future developments. I worked enthusiastically under him but achieved no distinguishing successes, mainly because I was young and was in Seattle for only six months. But my first experience overseas was a valuable education. Also, one person I met while in Seattle, Tojiro Okamoto, was later to influence the course of my entire life, for he introduced me some years later to Kiichiro Toyoda, the founder of Toyota Motor Company. I met Okamoto when he was working in the Seattle Office of Toyo Menka Kaisha, Ltd., a trading concern in the Mitsui group. I have always thought myself fortunate to have won his friendship.

In early 1919 I was transferred from Seattle to London, then the company's largest office overseas. I had heard that business there was good, and when I arrived the post-World War I economic boom was in full swing. The office manager was Tadaharu Mukai, who later became chairman of Mitsui & Co., and eventually Minister of Finance. My assignment was to the Iron and Steel Division, where I was put in charge of purchasing iron and steel. The next few years passed quickly. My responsibilities and authority increased, and work became more interesting.

After being in Mitsui about five years, however, I began thinking more seriously about my future. I knew that Mitsui tended to emphasize an employee's academic and family background when making promotions, and since I had come from neither a prominent university nor a prominent family I knew that while I might be promoted I certainly could never become a top executive. I felt somehow that life was much too short to be wasted by not developing myself to the fullest, and I began thinking that quitting Mitsui was the first step I had to take if I was to work toward satisfying my ambitions. By September 1923, the month that the Great Kanto Earthquake struck Tokyo and threw our office into great commotion, I had already nearly decided to resign. In July 1924 I was ordered back to Tokyo, and on the way home aboard ship I thought carefully about my options. Once back home I talked with my superiors, and I resigned from Mitsui & Co. in September. I then stayed in Japan until the following March, when I returned to London, this time to start my own trading company.

My return voyage to London in March 1925 was pleasant. Before leaving Japan I had mixed feelings of hope and doubt, but once at sea I relaxed. I remember sunning myself on deck and dreaming an impossible dream — how I would compete in England on an equal footing with Mitsui for world trade. And when I stepped ashore in London I put my luggage down, took a deep breath, and braced myself for the start of what I knew was going to be a difficult time.

Immediately after I arrived I set to work, and in April

Great Kanto Earthquake (1923). This earthquake caused wide destruction, particularly in Tokyo. The automobile played an important role during recovery and impressed people with its worth as a means of transport.

See p. 102, Col. A, "Great Kanto Earthquake" and p. 104, Col. A, "Heavy Inflow of Foreign Capital."

Shotaro Kamiya in London (c. 1925-26). An independent businessman, president of Kamiya Trading.

1925 I founded Kamiya Trading Company as an iron and steel wholesaler. Establishing the company was not very difficult, and at first I was the only employee. I rented one room for an office and after a while hired a typist to do my billing and general office work. My business was mainly the exporting of iron to Japan and brass to India. Kamiya Trading got off to a very good start: worldwide economic conditions were good, and I won orders from customers in London with whom I had had friendly business relations while in Mitsui. In fact, success made me so blind that for a time I really believed I could surpass Mitsui.

But world economic conditions changed. Japan's economic future turned bleak from around 1926 and the country raced headlong into an era of confusion and financial panic. In England, a large-scale, drawn-out strike by coalminers seriously affected the export of iron and steel. This worsening of the business environment came much too quickly and harshly for me, for I was operating on very little capital. I began to cut all my expenses, even gradually cutting food expenses, but business worsened steadily. Finally, while lying awake one night thinking, I decided to close Kamiya Trading. I judged circumstances to be against me, and realized that pride and determination were not enough to carry me through the difficult economic situation. It would be better to forget the past while I still could and to start completely fresh in some new field.

Closing Kamiya Trading was a turning point in my life. There is no way of knowing what would have happened if I had not gone out of business, of course, but at the very least I think that if I had kept Kamiya Trading alive my life would have been much more trying than the life I have led working in the automobile industry. However, I learned two important lessons from my business failure in 1927: I learned not to fret over mistakes, and not to struggle against the tide of events. I

24

learned to judge the existing state of affairs and to act according to my own judgment of the future. My experience made me think of the old saying, "Fall down seven times, get up eight times."

My dream of surpassing Mitsui thus ended without much fanfare, and in May 1927 I left London and headed home. I had no idea of what I would do after getting home, but I was still single, and only twenty-nine, and I felt that things would somehow work out. My optimism let me enjoy the trip home as much as I had enjoyed the trip abroad two years earlier.

When I arrived back in Japan financial panic had already struck. The famous bankruptcy of Suzuki Shoten Company, the collapse of the stock market and other events had thrown the economy into chaos. In the midst of the chaos, however, I learned that a number of foreign companies, including American automobile companies, were competing fiercely to expand their business in the Japanese market.

See p. 102, Col. B, "Start of Japan's Motorization," p. 104, Col. A, "Economic Chaos Prior to Great Depression" and p. 104, Col. A, "Japanese Society after Mid-1920s."

Chapter Two

Dawning of Japan's Auto Industry

After reaching Japan I went to spend some time with my family in Nagoya. I was there only a short while, however, before I began thinking again about work. Without capital I knew I could not possibly start another company, and my alternative therefore was to inquire around for work, even though I had told myself when I left Mitsui that I would never work again for a company. My failure in business had taught me that sometimes it is necessary to forget one's pride.

The two companies I decided to approach were Ford-Japan and GM-Japan. Both had knock-down assembly operations in Japan, Ford in Yokohama and General Motors in Osaka. Business for both was growing and they were competing as fiercely in Japan as they were in the United States. Besides their good

See p. 102, Col. B, "Ford-Japan and GM-Japan."

business, there were other reasons for my decision to approach these two companies. I had an interest in automobiles that dated from my first stay in London with Mitsui. The British motor car industry was just then being developed, mainly through Wolseley, Morris and others, and I had become interested in the industry after talking with friends and customers in England about the future of the automobile. One English friend in particular was highly enthusiastic about the automobile, and I remember how we used to talk for hours about the coming automobile age. Also, I wanted to work for a foreign company in order to use my overseas experience and my English.

Armed with a letter of recommendation from Mitsui, I applied to Ford and to General Motors. They surprised me because within a week I received favorable replies from both, probably because of my experience in Seattle and London and because of my English. General Motors offered me a monthly salary of 300 yen and Ford 500 yen, exceptionally good salaries at the time. Work for GM would be in Osaka, and work for Ford would be in Tokyo. But Ford set one difficult condition: though I would be accepted immediately for employment, I would have to wait a few months to begin work. When I asked how long "a few months" would be, Ford said at least six months. Later I learned that Ford was in the process of replacing the Model-T with the Model-A.

General Motors asked me to begin work immediately. For my part, I knew neither company very well and I had no special preference. Ford offered the better salary, but I felt that six months was too long to be without a job. Also, during my GM interview I sensed that I had compatible views with the company's general manager for Japan, and I thus decided to work for GM.

That is how I entered the automobile business, beginning with General Motors in January 1928, almost fifty years ago.

Model-A Ford (1928). Produced to compete with the Chevrolet.

The thought that so many years have passed so quickly amazes me, and certainly I never imagined when I joined GM-Japan that I would spend the rest of my life in the automobile business. Moreover, no thought of Toyota was in my mind then, for Toyota Motor Company had not yet even been founded. Nor was there any possible way to guess that the Japanese automobile industry would develop as it later did. Only 347 domestic-made vehicles and 24,314 knocked-down imports were produced in Japan in 1928. Total registrations that year were only 66,777 vehicles, slightly more than the country's 59,200 rickshaws.

General Motors had grown rapidly in the United States during the 1920s, largely because it followed a policy of offering consumers a full line of vehicles. Ford Motor Company, on the other hand, relied too heavily on its Model-T and thus fell behind GM. GM first outpaced Ford's sales in the American market in 1927, the same year that it began operations in Japan. Ford by then had already been in Japan three years, and thus had a good headstart in the Japanese market. But it seemed only a matter of time before General Motors would surpass Ford in sales in Japan just as it had done in the United States. GM offices were busy, and even young Japanese employees were given much authority.

My first assignment was to the Osaka Head Office's Sales and Publicity Department, which was in charge of dealer outlets, sales planning, advertising and publicity. I was somewhat disappointed on my first day at work because I was asked to check and file sales slips, but I was happy to be in the department I had requested.

The automobile business was new to me and I had to work hard. At the end of my first year I was appointed assistant manager of the department, and after another year I became department manager, the highest post any Japanese had in the company in 1930. Such a swift rise was unheard of in Japanese companies, but it was possible in General Motors because the company based promotions on performance rather than seniority, school or family background. I had left Mitsui precisely because it emphasized school and family backgrounds in making promotions and I was therefore quite happy with GM's policy. Not long after becoming manager of the Sales and Publicity

Kamiya as Manager of GM's Tokyo Office (1930).

Department, I was also appointed manager of the Tokyo Office and moved to Tokyo.

Economic conditions in Japan were still bad. And since business was having trouble recovering from the financial chaos of the late 1920s, the government moved to promote the rationalization of industry, with the Ministry of Commerce and Industry directing operations. In 1931 the Ministry set up a Committee for the Establishment of the Automobile Industry, which then began preparing proposals. Until then the military had been administering the industry, and reverting its administration back to civilian authority indicated not only a recognition of the poor economic conditions but also the recognition that the automobile industry was indeed a vital industry.

As manager of the Tokyo Office of General Motors, I was considered an expert on automobiles, and the Ministry of Commerce and Industry often asked me for advice and for information on the automobile industry. In the end, however, the committee made no proposals for promoting the motor vehicle industry in Japan; and after the Manchurian Incident of 1931 and the Shanghai Incident of 1932 the administration of the automobile industry reverted again to the military. The military subsequently prepared aggressive plans concerning development of the automobile industry, for it needed a large number of trucks for operations on the Asian continent and also wanted to prepare a motor vehicle supply system in case war broke out. A clear expression of the military's determination was the Law Concerning the Manufacture of Motor Vehicles, promulgated in May 1936.

Just as the Ministry of Commerce and Industry had asked me for information on the automobile industry, so did the Ministry of War. From my contacts with the latter I gained a good understanding of the international situation as Japan viewed it and of trends in the government's thinking regarding the automobile industry.

See p. 106, Col. A, "Manchurian and Shanghai Incidents," p. 106, Col. B, "Committee for Establishment of Automobile Industry" and p. 108, Col. B, "Law Concerning Manufacture of Motor Vehicles."

Meanwhile, General Motors was also very interested in policy changes that the Japanese government was considering that might affect its business, and headquarters in Detroit instructed GM-Japan to keep them informed. As manager of the Tokyo Office it was my responsibility to collect and forward information to Detroit, and my position thus was awkward, for while such information was not secret it obviously related directly to national defense. Frankly, I hesitated to cooperate in providing such information, even though I worked for GM, and this conflict led me to consider resigning.

When Japan's economy finally began recovering from the poor business conditions of the late 1920s and early 1930s, the upturn was fast, stimulated especially by activity in the defense industries. By dropping out of the League of Nations in 1933 and scrapping the Washington Disarmament Treaty in 1934, the Japanese government made it even more difficult to avoid open war. At the end of 1934, as the international political situation was worsening almost daily, I was transferred back to GM's Head Office in Osaka.

I was appointed assistant manager of the Head Office, but though the transfer meant a promotion I did not want to leave Tokyo, the country's political and economic center. Moreover, General Motors at the time was negotiating for a tie-up with Nissan Motor Company, newly established in December 1933, and I was in charge of the negotiations. I regretted leaving Tokyo before the talks were completed. GM had hoped that a tie-up with Nissan would let it survive in Japan even if regulations were tightened on foreign companies. As it turned out the negotiations were stopped not long after I left Tokyo.

After assuming my post in Osaka I began thinking seriously about leaving GM and joining a Japanese auto manufacturer. I thought more about it each day, for the government was openly promoting the domestic industry and the future for imported cars had began to look bleak after the administration of the motor industry was transferred back to the Ministry of War. The government gradually restricted the importation of automobiles in order to protect the domestic auto industry and to bring equilibrium to Japan's balance of international payments. Government records show that the number of imported cars reached a peak of 34,556 in 1929 then fell to 15,573 in 1933. GM-Japan's number of knock-down cars dropped from 15,745 in 1929 to 5,942 in 1933 — almost a two-thirds drop.

Besides these various practical reasons, my personal feelings toward the Americans in GM also made me consider leaving. I am not sure whether or not to call my feelings "nationalistic," but I certainly did feel some dissatisfaction toward the American staff of GM. I felt that their attitude then toward the Japanese staff was much colder than simple economic rationalism might dictate.

Their policy toward dealers was especially merciless, and almost daily they cut ties with dealers in financial trouble. I remember thinking that while such action might be accepted business practice in the United States, where companies rely greatly on written contracts, customs are different in Japan and GM officers should try to understand the local situation more. I often complained to the American staff and tried to persuade them to help dealers instead of dropping them, especially since I visited dealers and knew firsthand their predicament. But GM ignored my complaints. It was at this time that I thought out one of my most important business principles, the necessity for coexistence and co-prosperity with dealers.

At about the time that I began to think about working for a Japanese auto manufacturer, I was informally approached by Nissan Motor Company, and that contact stimulated my thinking still more. I also heard that Toyoda Automatic Loom Works was planning to enter the motor industry. Before making any final decision about quitting GM I wanted to hear more about Toyoda. If Toyoda looked hopeful I thought I

Tojiro Okamoto (1889-   ). Okamoto arranged the first meeting between Kamiya and Kiichiro Toyoda.

might apply there for work because the company was near my hometown and I could commute easily. So while on a trip home I stopped in Nagoya City to visit Tojiro Okamoto and ask about Toyoda's plans. I had made Okamoto's acquaintance while in Seattle, as I mentioned earlier. I had learned that he was manager of Toyoda Spinning and Weaving Company and a confidant of Kiichiro Toyoda, the man in Toyoda Automatic Loom Works in charge of the Automotive Department. Of course I never expected that my visit to Okamoto's home, made on the spur of the moment, would lead to a lifetime relationship with Toyoda.

Okamoto was quite surprised by my unannounced visit, but he welcomed me warmly as an old friend. Sixteen years had passed since I had last seen him. We talked about what we had been doing over the years and then I asked him about Toyoda's plans regarding the automobile business, about the progress it was making, and about its sales policies. Okamoto said that while he knew no details he did know that Kiichiro Toyoda was working very hard to enter the new industry and that while Toyoda was making considerable progress in manufacturing it

Sakichi Toyoda (1867-1930). Foremost Japanese inventor, and founder of Toyota.

was troubled by problems in marketing. Okamoto advised me to meet and talk with Kiichiro, and I told him that was exactly what I had hoped to be able to do. He telephoned Kiichiro, and Kiichiro suggested that we meet that night in Nagoya.

Events thus moved very quickly, and I was excited by the idea of meeting the eldest son of Sakichi Toyoda, the famous inventor, founder of the giant Toyoda family group, and a leading figure in business circles of central Japan. I was nervous at first but felt immediately at ease after meeting Kiichiro, for he was obviously a humble and honest man. He spoke about how badly he wanted to produce domestic cars, and while his speech was not eloquent his sincerity was real. He surprised me especially when he said that he had good engineers and could produce cars but that he had no marketing staff and could not sell them. He said that if I joined Toyoda he would let me make all marketing decisions.

His generous offer took me aback, as did the progress of our talks. I had not yet definitely decided to leave GM, and I visited Okamoto merely to ask about Toyoda's plans so that I could make a wiser decision about my future. I told Kiichiro I

See p. 101, Col. C, "Sakichi Toyoda (1867-1930)."

Kiichiro Toyoda (1894-1952). Devoted his entire life to developing wholly domestic-made automobiles. Second president of Toyota Motor Company.

wanted a little time to decide, and I asked him if I could visit the Toyoda plant. Kiichiro wanted to go to the plant at once, but it was late and we agreed instead to go the next day.

When I went the next morning with Kiichiro to the Toyoda Automatic Loom Works, located at Kariya, I was surprised again. I had heard that Toyoda was working on a prototype vehicle, but there were ten or more trucks there. Kiichiro showed me around the plant, explaining at the same time that it was a temporary facility and that he was planning a permanent one. He also said that his real aim was to develop a small-size passenger car, although he was then working on trucks. My impression of Kiichiro at our first meeting, coupled with my impression of the plant, made me admire him greatly. His goals, his zeal and his character told me that he was a man I could work hard for. I said I would accept his offer of a job.

The next day I went back to Nagoya and met Noboru Yamaguchi, the late Manager of Hinode Motors and President of Aichi Toyota Motor Company. I told Yamaguchi of my decision to join Toyoda. Hinode Motors was a leading GM dealer, and Yamaguchi and I had become good friends and had

· See p. 103, Col. C, "Toyoda Automatic Loom Works, Ltd."

Koromo Plant (today's Honsha Plant) under construction. Completed in September 1938, this plant in Koromo (today's Toyota City) was the first of Toyota's eight major plants.

developed a mutual respect beyond our business relationship. Yamaguchi encouraged me in my decision and said that if I went to Toyoda he was willing to have Hinode Motors surrender its GM dealership in exchange for a Toyoda one. Like me, he was disappointed with GM's harsh dealer policies then, and he told me that he also had been thinking about working with a domestic manufacturer. My talk with him made me all the more determined.

From Nagoya I went to Osaka and talked about my decision with two of my subordinates in the Sales and Publicity Department — Kanosuke Hanasaki, late Managing Director of Toyota Motor Sales Company, and Seisi Kato, now President of Toyota Motor Sales Company. Both were eager to join me in my move to Toyoda.

Chapter Three

Marketing Domestic-made Vehicles

When I turned in my resignation to General Motors, the general manager asked me why I would want to give up such an exceptionally high position and good salary. When I said that I was going to join Toyoda to sell domestic-made cars, he was even more surprised. It was hard to explain why I would leave a high position in GM-Japan in order to sell cars that existed only on the drawing board. But I told him that I sincerely wanted to devote myself to building a domestic car industry. I did not care so much about the personal cost if I could contribute to my country's development. I left GM amicably.

Kiichiro and I had not discussed my salary before I joined Toyoda, and only afterward did I discover that it was only 120 yen a month. I had thus accepted a four-fifths cut from my GM salary of 600 yen. Since my salary equalled that of the directors of the company, however, and since I had not joined Toyoda for more money, I did not complain. I warned Hanazaki and Kato in Osaka that their salaries would be considerably lower if they joined Toyoda, but they decided to come anyway.

The Automotive Department of Toyoda Automatic Loom Works was preparing to exhibit its first vehicle, the Model G-1 truck, in Tokyo at the end of November. No one knew that the company had already begun manufacturing, and the Tokyo show thus would be a formal declaration that the company had entered the motor industry. I played a major role in preparing the show, and I had to reexamine everything that had already been done because no one else had any experience. Kiichiro had warned me so, but I still threw up my hands in despair.

I told Kiichiro about Hanazaki and Kato around this time and he told me again that he trusted my judgment in all sales matters and that if I wanted them he would hire them. I sent a telegram telling them to come to Nagoya but to be prepared for the worst.

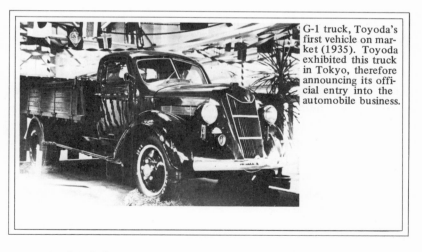

G-1 truck, Toyoda's first vehicle on market (1935). Toyoda exhibited this truck in Tokyo, therefore announcing its official entry into the automobile business.

See p. 107, Col. C, "Into Automobile Industry" and p. 109, Col. C, "Toyoda's First Marketed Motor Vehicle, Model G-1 Truck."

The show introducing the Toyoda G-1 truck was held in the Tokyo Automobile Hotel on the 21st and 22nd of November 1935. Forty years have passed since then and I suppose now it is alright to talk about the quality of the vehicles we showed. I heard from Seisi Kato, who was part of the group that transported the trucks from Kariya to Tokyo, that they ran into countless problems along the way. There were mechanical breakdowns, and engine adjustments had to be made during rest periods all the way to Tokyo.

The show, however, was a complete success. In order to advertise our truck, we invited people from the Home Ministry, the Ministry of Commerce and Industry, the Ministry of War, the Railway Ministry and other government offices. Some people say that our show and Toyoda's formal entry into the motor industry encouraged the military to push for enactment of the Law Concerning the Manufacture of Motor Vehicles, for the military advocated the early establishment of a wholly domestic motor vehicle production industry. But it was never Toyoda's deliberate intention to influence the military.

The ex-factory price of the G-1 truck we exhibited was 2,900 yen, lower by 200 yen than Ford or Chevrolet trucks. I set the price because Kiichiro had no idea of how to decide it. That price meant selling at a loss, but Kiichiro consented when I explained to him that this was common automobile marketing strategy. I told him that we could not expect to expand our sales rapidly with only a patriotic appeal to buy domestic-made vehicles. We had to raise demand by supplying vehicles in the market cheaply, and after demand increased we could then produce in volume and reach a break-even point.

Our success in Tokyo encouraged us, but many problems remained as we moved to put our trucks on the market. We had no sales network at all, for example, and it was my responsibility to establish one.

My first move in establishing our dealer network was a visit

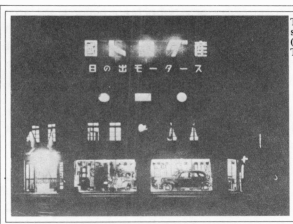

Toyoda's first dealer-
ship: Hinode Motors
(today's Aichi
Toyota) (1935).

to Noboru Yamaguchi of Hinode Motors in Nagoya. He had told me he would accept a Toyoda dealership and I visited him with an offer, which he immediately accepted. Then he set out to persuade hesitant employees that the move to Toyoda would be wise. In late 1935 Hinode Motors returned its Buick dealer-ship to General Motors, and started afresh as the first Toyoda dealer.

On December 8, 1935, Toyoda held its first hometown show in the showroom of Hinode Motors. While the Tokyo show was a kind of public announcement, the Nagoya show was for selling, an important difference. And because Nagoya was Toyoda's hometown, the show was well-attended and Toyoda was given enthusiastic support by people of the region. But the enthusiastic reception made the sales people ill at ease, for they wondered if our product's quality was equal to our customers' enthusiasm.

I heard from Yamaguchi afterward that the rear axle housing of one truck sent to the exhibition broke when the vehicle lightly brushed a streetlight pole on the way to the showroom. Another vehicle was sent to replace it, which calmed most fears, but when Risaburo Toyoda, who later became the first president of Toyota Motor Company, arrived at the showroom and was introduced to Yamaguchi, the first thing he asked was whether the trucks' wheels were going around okay. His question struck fear in everyone on the sales staff.

I told Yamaguchi that it was important to develop an exceptionally good after-sales service system. We had to provide a complete maintenance guarantee in order to reassure our customers. We could not fail in our duty to give good after-sales service to customers who wanted to give domestic-made vehicles a try. Toyota's policy of giving top priority to customers was first implemented then.

After the show at Hinode Motors we had to begin establishing a nationwide sales network. I proposed establishing dealer outlets using local capital and local managers. There were arguments against my proposal — doubts about the extent to which outside capital would be helpful, and fears that if dealers gave up halfway we would be left with no options. Some people recommended building a system of dealers under direct management, but Kiichiro supported my proposal.

I thought that the most effective way to establish a network quickly was to convince dealers of imported cars to join Toyoda and sell domestic cars, although it was certainly not as easy to persuade others as it was to persuade Hinode Motors. Toyoda still was not widely known and had no products which could show its technology proudly. There was nothing to do but explain to prospective dealers the need to promote the domestic industry and ask them to have confidence in Toyoda. Fortunately, dealers began to accept our ideas, and our circumstances turned favorable. In about one year we established eight dealerships.

While working to establish this small network, I worked out more clearly my principle of mutual coexistence and co-prosperity with dealers. Toyoda could achieve its goals only with

See p. 111, Col. C, "Establishment of a Franchise System — Preparing a Sales Network."

the cooperation of local dealers using their own capital. Our prosperity depended on their prosperity, and if they gave up on us halfway we could not possibly succeed. One of the reasons why some car dealers had turned to Toyoda was that they did not like GM's policies toward the development of local capital. Dealers would not cooperate fully if we considered them merely as channels for selling our products. I believe that the ideal relation between a manufacturer and its dealers is for both to profit; that is, prosperous coexistence.

In May 1936, just three months after the historic February 26th Incident, the government enacted the Law Concerning the Manufacture of Motor Vehicles in order to establish a system of domestic automobile manufacturing. Under that new law the production of motor vehicles came under government control. In September 1936 Toyoda Automatic Loom Works became the first company under that law to be given a production license. The law also made the sale of imported cars more difficult and the sale of domestic cars easier. Moreover, the government began making stronger demands for promotion of the domestic industry, and Toyoda's responsibility grew heavier.

41

Kiichiro Toyoda established Toyota Motor Company by separating the Automotive Department from Toyoda Automatic Loom Works in August 1937. The new company started full-scale manufacturing of motor vehicles, inheriting from the original company all the facilities connected with auto production. Risaburo Toyoda was chosen as the company's first president because of his influential position in the Toyoda family, and Kiichiro became vice-president, though in fact he made all final decisions. Recommended by Kiichiro, I became a director and manager of the sales department, although I had been with Toyoda for only two years. When organizing the new sales department, I reflected back on my experience in GM-Japan. I did not want our sales department to be merely a business

See p. 106, Col. A, "February 26th Incident," p. 108, Col. B, "Automobile Industry and Wartime Preparations" and p. 109, Col. C, "Establishment of Toyota Motor Company."

Risaburo Toyoda (1884-1952). First president of Toyota Motor Company.

department; I wanted it to be a center of mutual cooperation between all parts of the Toyota network, from the manufacturer, to the dealer, to the customer.

Kiichiro told me that he wanted eventually to sell 2,000 cars per month, and I told him that credit sales would be necessary and that a finance company was needed to support such sales. I pointed out that GM-Japan and Ford-Japan had already established finance companies back in 1929 and were conducting credit sales. In October 1939 Kiichiro established Toyoda Finance, the predecessor of Toyoda Tsusho Kaisha, a finance company still operating today, and we introduced a twelve-month installment buying system in order to compete with General Motors and Ford.

Thus Toyota gradually built an over-all structure for large-scale production and sales, and its output in 1939 exceeded 10,000 vehicles. However, wartime controls were already being extended in 1939 to the production and selling of motor vehicles. Controls at first were only on production, but in May they were also set on sales, and in October government price controls were introduced. Large trucks and buses came under distribution controls in August 1940, and small trucks and electric buses were included in November.

In December 1941 the Motorcar Control Commission was established, and in July 1942, under that Commission, the Japan Motorcar Distribution System (Nippai) was established; next, in November 1942, the Regional Automotive Maintenance and Distribution Corporation (Jihai) was established. These two systems united all the dealers of Toyota, Nissan and Diesel Kogyo. The Nippai collected all motor vehicles produced by manufacturers and distributed them to the Jihai, which then distributed them to customers. Free competition was no longer possible, and though I was against these developments, I was powerless to stop them. In fact I was obliged to become a

Wartime regulations affected sales and production of motor vehicles. As sales manager of Toyota, Kamiya had to win the understanding of high military officials (at Toyota Motor Company, 1938).

managing director of the Nippai and manager of the Vehicles Department, which made me responsible for the over-all collection and distribution of vehicles. I was fortunate because I met many competent people in the Jihai system and established good relations with them, many of whom joined Toyota after the war.

The war, meanwhile, gradually turned against Japan, and the army was pushed back daily at the front. In January 1944, moreover, Toyota Motor Company was designated a military facility. We heard militarists shouting their slogans louder than ever, but Japan was about to awake from a nightmare in which countless lives had been lost.

The war ended on August 15, 1945. Almost the entire nation listened to the Emperor's recorded message of surrender on the radio, and every Japanese who heard it must have experienced a profound, indescribable emotion, for the Emperor told us that Japan had been defeated in war for the first time in history. Confusion in the country was great, and no one knew really what to expect. I was uneasy, too, of course, and yet I felt some hope because the end of the war might mean the end of government controls and the start of a period in which Japan could rebuild herself in a freely competitive situation. This hope prompted me suddenly to take off my drab national uniform and don my cambric suit from the corner of the highboy where it had been hanging for years.

The General Headquarters of the Supreme Commander for the Allied Powers, which we all called GHQ, was sympathetic toward the needs of the automobile industry in Japan, undoubtedly because it was headed mainly by Americans, and the United States was the world's major automobile producing country. Although GHQ at first continued the wartime ban on the manufacture of motor vehicles, it immediately recognized that Japan's recovery would be impossible without efficient transportation, and less than six weeks after the surrender, on

See p. 110, Col. A, "August 15, 1945 – End of War."

September 25, 1945, the authorities partially lifted the ban and allowed total monthly production of 1,500 trucks. But materials were scarce, and the automobile distribution and marketing systems remained under controls. Toyota's business was not good, and financing was especially difficult. Money for production and sales had to be borrowed from the Reconstruction Finance Bank.

I had returned to Toyota in November 1944, after three years in the Nippai, and by the time I was promoted to Managing Director, in December 1945, I had already begun working particularly hard to persuade GHQ to remove all its restrictions from the marketing of automobiles. Fortunately, I was in a good position, having been appointed, together with Genshichi Asahara of Nissan Motor Company, as an adviser from the automobile industry to GHQ. I was in frequent contact with GHQ officials, and I explained conditions in the Japanese automobile industry to them. I assisted them sometimes in policy-making decisions.

One of the military officials responsible for making the final decision to remove marketing restrictions was a Major Bunting (phonetic). He was very familiar with the American automobile industry and had a clear understanding of the automobile sales system I thought that Japan needed. However, times being what they were meant that we had to wait. But I was confident that the franchise system which I proposed — a sales system organized by manufacturers — would be approved eventually. I continued to press Bunting and at the same time started preparations for reorganizing Toyota's sales network.

I was convinced that the dissolution of the Jihai would give Toyota an excellent chance to employ a highly competent sales staff. The leading Toyota and Nissan dealers had gone to the Jihai, as well as many other men experienced in automobile sales. And since the Jihai was neither controlled by nor affiliated with any particular maker, its members had no personal

See p. 110, Col. A, "Reconstruction Finance Bank."

Major Bunting of GHQ at Toyota Motor Company (1946). Bunting understood the problems the Japanese automobile industry faced.

outside obligations. If the Jihai were dissolved, however, and if its members resumed their former affiliations, we could not ethically recruit them into Toyota; but while they were still in the Jihai it was perfectly ethical to ask them to join Toyota later. Experience had taught me that a strong automobile marketing organization is closely related to staff competence, and so I tried to persuade as many persons in the Jihai as possible to commit themselves to Toyota.

Actually, GHQ made its final decision earlier than I had expected, possibly because Major Bunting agreed with my ideas about the automobile industry and moved to have them implemented. At any rate, on June 18, 1946, the Transport Ministry, in the name of the Director of the Land Transport

Bureau, issued a GHQ-approved memorandum for improving the automobile distribution system, stipulating that the Jihai was to be dissolved and that dealers could serve as distributors for the manufacturer of their choice. I had been preparing for this event for about a month.

I had discussed with Kiichiro earlier my belief that the approaching dissolution of the Jihai would afford us a rare chance to strengthen our sales network if we explained Toyota's thinking beforehand to competent people in the Jihai. Kiichiro agreed with me and contacted Jihai representatives all over the country, inviting them to attend a meeting in Toyota's main office in Koromo (now Toyota City) on May 18, 1946. As it turned out, that meeting was held one month to the day prior to the Jihai's dissolution.

Kiichiro gave the main address at the meeting, a talk about Japan's present automotive industry and Toyota's future, stressing the possibilities for growth in the automobile industry and the hopes and plans of Toyota. Then I talked about Toyota's marketing strategy and sales system, and gave an outline of our thinking about franchising. I do not remember everything I said, but records show that I commented partly as follows:

... while the growth of the American automobile industry has been due to modernized research and production facilities, no less important to its growth has been the personal experience of American carowners with particular automobiles. Although we in the Japanese auto industry must recognize the vital importance of technological improvements, we must not neglect sales policies that keep in mind the interests of our customers. Automobile manufacturers cannot exist without dealers, and dealers cannot exist without customers; these are the two tenets which guide the American auto industry. And they are the reasons why car dealers in the United States are organized directly under car manufacturers. In reaching the high growth level it has, the American auto industry has accumulated valuable experiences, and it behooves us in Japan to learn from those experiences. After studying our marketing policy for the future, therefore, we at Toyota have decided, given the approval of the authorities concerned, to establish a system of operating directly with our dealers, as we did before the war and as is done now in the United States.

When referring to the approval of "the authorities concerned," of course, I was actually saying that GHQ was preparing to permit a franchise system in the distribution of automobiles. I also remember expressing at Koromo my belief that the customer comes first, the dealer second, and the manufacturer last. What I said was not new to people at the meeting who had been with Toyota in prewar days, but most of the people who had been with other companies were apparently surprised. I was told later by one non-Toyota man that Kiichiro's grand vision and my emphasis on respect for the dealer inspired many men from other companies to join Toyota.

Looking back on the early postwar years, I now realize how important the Koromo meeting in May 1946 was for bringing many capable people into Toyota who contributed much toward the company's later growth.

Some preparations for reorganizing our sales network were thus already made when the Jihai was abolished according to the June 18th memorandum. Since we had begun preparing sooner than other companies, and since we had spoken to dealers about our future plans, the remodelling of our sales network proceeded smoothly; we were aided especially by Noboru Yamaguchi and by other dealers from the old Toyota group. On November 16, 1946, the Toyota Motor Sales Union (renamed the Toyota Motor Sales Dealers Association on May

26, 1948) was established. It gave a strong, new push to the company's sales network. Toyota Motor Company and the Sales Union pledged to work together to prepare for a dawning age of free competition.

In establishing the new sales network, I was most concerned about ensuring good relations between Toyota's regular people and Toyota's new people who had been at Nissan previously. One idea I had was to appoint someone from the old Nissan group as Board Chairman of the Sales Union. The regular Toyota people deserving that position, such as Noboru Yamaguchi, appreciated my idea, and thus the first appointment of Board Chairman went to a former Nissan man, Takesaburo Kikuchi. We also made other appointments in the Sales Union that would show everyone the importance we attached to unified cooperation. While our sales network was a mixed group at first, it soon became a single unit working for a common purpose. And as industrial materials became more available, Toyota Motor Company began to grow. Dealers gradually strengthened their own sales organizations, and the future began to look bright.

Yet we soon discovered that recovery from the devastations of war was not quite so simple. In order to finance our dealers we eventually had to establish a completely new sales company, mainly because the Reconstruction Finance Bank stopped granting us loans.

See p. 113, Col. C, "Passenger Car Production Begins Again."

Chapter Four

Toyota Motor Sales Company

In 1949 GHQ instituted a new economic policy, popularly called the "Dodge Line." It was a heavy blow to Japanese industry because it called for financial retrenchment and a halt to reconstruction financing, and it hurt the auto industry badly.

About this same time, a slump in new car sales and delays in the collection of time payments on credit sales were forcing Toyota Motor Company into a serious liquidity crisis, thereby adding to the difficulties caused by GHQ's new policy. I remember how busy we were trying to promote sales and collect credits, but the Dodge Line produced rampant inflation which none of us could do anything to stop, and Toyota Motor Company found itself with a critical need for ¥200 million in cash at the end of December 1949.

See p. 112, Col. A, "Dodge Line."

This liquidity crisis was resolved mainly thanks to the good judgment of and help from Takeo Takanashi, then Director of the Bank of Japan's Nagoya District Office. Takanashi believed that Toyota and its more than 300 subsidiaries were so important to industry in the Nagoya area that Toyota deserved financing from the Bank of Japan. He won support for his views and Toyota borrowed the funds it needed from a consortium of twenty-four banks, headed by the Teikoku and Tokai Banks. While this cash let Toyota meet its year-end obligations, one of the conditions of the loan was that the Company had to revise drastically its reconstruction plan, beginning immediately. This condition provided the main stimulus for establishing Toyota Motor Sales Company, and for rethinking the basic outline of Toyota's over-all management policy for the subsequent two decades. The age-old saying that "luck and misfortune are intertwined like twisted strands of a rope" certainly held true for Toyota.

In arranging Toyota's loan, the Bank of Japan in Nagoya drew up a three-point plan for reconstructing the Company. First, that the Sales Department would be separated from Toyota Motor Company and be made into an independent company. Second, that the number of automobiles Toyota produces not exceed the number the new sales company was confident of selling. Third, that unnecessary employees be reduced to a minimum. The Bank of Japan and the city banks in the loan syndicate judged that Toyota's financial problems came from an overly bullish managerial policy regarding production which led to costly inventories. Unless this management attitude were changed, the banks said, Toyota could not possibly become financially independent again, no matter how many loans it received.

Toyota Motor Company then began designing its reconstruction along the lines of the Bank of Japan's three-point plan. I was appointed the Company's chief representative for negotiating details with the loan syndicate for separating the Sales Department — that is, for establishing Toyota Motor Sales Company.

For some time up to then I had advocated establishing an independent sales company, but my concept and the concept the banks held were different. The banks wanted the sales company mainly to assume a financial function while I wanted it to assume a marketing function. Actually, Toyota Motor Company on three previous occasions had studied the feasibility of setting up a sales company. The first occasion was in June 1946 — just before dissolution of the Jihai — the second was in April 1947, and the third in May 1948. Toyota was unable to make any final decision at those times because of GHQ's changing economic policies. But the results of the earlier studies were available to me and they proved quite useful for working out plans to establish the new company in 1950.

The earlier studies let me review and prepare the Company's position, and therefore I was able to assert an independent stance when I negotiated with the banks. Thus, while the immediate stimulus for establishing the sales company was pressure to do so from the banks, Toyota had pretty much its own say in the negotiations and had its views fully reflected in the final agreement.

Toyota left the selection of the new company's president to the Bank of Japan, which, along with the consortium, asked me to assume the post. But setting up the company proved more difficult than I had expected, mostly because of unforeseen obstacles in financing and in various legal restrictions. Under a SCAP directive issued on December 8, 1945, entitled "Schedule of Restricted Concerns," Toyota Motor Company became a "restricted concern," which meant that the Company, its executives and its employees were prohibited from investing in the new sales company. This forced us to go outside Toyota for the funds the new company needed. Initially, we hoped to

52

See p. 112, Col. A, "GHQ Directive Concerning Restricted Concerns" and p. 115, Col. C, "Establishment of Toyota Motor Sales Company."

borrow at least ¥100 million, but after exhausting all possible sources I was able to raise only ¥80 million, including investment in kind on products. This amount became the initial paid-up capitalization of Toyota Motor Sales Company.

Other difficulties resulted from legal restrictions. We not only had to be careful about violating the anti-monopoly law and the directive on restricted concerns but also had to tread gingerly before the complex requirements of the Security and Exchange Law and the Commerce Law.

Registration of the new company was completed on April 3, 1950. April 1 was the start of the new fiscal year, but we had to wait until July 1 to begin operations because labor troubles broke out at Toyota Motor Company.

First and only labor dispute at Toyota Motor Company (1950).

Perhaps it was inevitable that employees would have to be laid off when we rebuilt Toyota Motor Company, but it was hard for a man like Kiichiro Toyoda to lay off anyone. At any rate, the labor union flatly rejected any cut in personnel and immediately organized a worker's struggle committee when it heard about proposed layoffs. The union began holding daily strikes, worker sabotages and protest meetings. Toyota was caught up in a whirlpool of confusion.

In a move to settle the strike, President Kiichiro Toyoda and all representative directors accepted responsibility and resigned en masse on June 5, 1950. A new president was appointed, Taizo Ishida, who had been president of Toyoda Automatic Loom Works for many years, and Fukio Nakagawa of the Teikoku Bank was appointed executive director. The situation improved thereafter, and after two months the dispute finally ended on June 9.

I was not directly involved in the labor dispute because I left Toyota Motor Company in order to head the new sales company, but I was very busy at the time soliciting the cooperation and assistance of various groups, particularly those in finance,

Taizo Ishida (1888-   ). President of Toyota Motor Company following the labor dispute in 1950. Played an important role in Toyota's reconstruction, and in building a firm foundation for the Company's growth.

See p. 115, Col. C, "Toyota's One and Only Labor Dispute, Wide-Scale Social Repercussions."

to support our efforts to make the new company a success.

Kiichiro Toyoda was to be reinstated as president as soon as Toyota's recovery was completed. Unfortunately, however, he passed away suddenly on March 27, 1952. His death was saddening to many, for he was well-known and highly respected. His death was especially painful to me because we had always been so close. I was probably his closest confidant in the long, hard task of developing Japan's automobile industry, and only once in the eighteen years I knew him had he become angry with me. It was when the Company was receiving complaints from dealers about leaking radiators. I believed we had to act immediately, and I said to Kiichiro, partly in jest, "How can I sell cars that have to run with buckets dangling under their radiators?" He turned almost furious. "In all my years as an engineer I have never been so insulted," he said. "I'll tell you what. If you stop selling cars, I'll stop making them." And before I could reply he left the room. I was dumbfounded, and ran after him, apologizing as I went, until finally he calmed down. Kiichiro Toyoda had trusted me completely, which was unusual since I had joined Toyota in mid-career and was, in that sense, an outsider. He always told me to do things the way I thought was best. My respect for him was immense, and I worked hard to live up to his expectations. When he died I vowed with new determination to develop a volume sales system that would help achieve his dream of a car for every Japanese family.

Toyota Motor Sales Company began all-out operations after the labor dispute at Toyota Motor Company was settled. But we were unable to bypass legal restrictions against taking over assets from Toyota Motor Company, and won only three rights: the right to transfer 358 employees to the new company, the right to use the Toyota trademark, and the right to do business in the facilities formerly used by Toyota Motor Company's sales department. Our fixed assets were zero; we were starting out with almost nothing.

I told myself at the time that while the Company had no fixed assets it did have a dependable staff, the greatest of all assets. If the Company took good care of its core of dedicated, capable men, they would work hard for us. This belief about personnel remains with me to this day.

I felt that we should develop the new Company so that eventually it could operate in all aspects of marketing. But priority in the early days was on finding ways to finance sales. To that end, we devised a new type of monthly installment plan.

Considering that the Company had only limited fund-raising power because of its low corporate credit rating, we thought of somehow using our product, the automobile, as collateral. More specifically, we wanted to have consumers sign monthly promissory notes which we could then use as collateral for bank loans.

The financial people were skeptical of the new plan, but we persisted until they were convinced of its safety and fairness. The Bank of Japan's Takeo Takanashi, the same man who had helped Toyota in late 1949, was especially helpful, and after he showed interest more banks gradually accepted our plan. Our fund-raising capacity for supporting sales grew quickly. Toyota Motor Company was thus able to concentrate on production, and we in sales — no longer troubled by cash problems — concentrated on improving our marketing system, especially on modernizing our dealer outlets.

SCAP had completely lifted its controls on automobile production on April 1, 1950, and an age of free competition seemed to have arrived. I was busy with an intensive study at that time for determining the best automobile sales system for Toyota. In June 1950, for example, Kiichiro sent me to the United States. While on that trip I became convinced that we not only had to push forward with our new installment

See p. 117, Col. C, "Monthly Installment Financing."

When Toyota decided in 1953 to develop completely domestic-made passenger car using its own technology, this SF sedan was only passenger car model it was producing (1951).

purchase system but that we also had to streamline our sales outlets, which meant firmly establishing a modern concept of sales for our marketing channels to the consumer. One way of ensuring consumer confidence was to make sure that our products did not seem too far removed from the manufacturer. Also, while it was important to lower prices in order to make our products more accessible, it was even more important to create an image of auto sales that would elicit popular confidence. Popular confidence was especially necessary because war had already started in Korea when I returned from the United States, and the demand by the U.N. Forces for Japanese goods was starting to stimulate the economy to the extent that more people would soon be purchasing cars.

In order to modernize our dealer outlets I drew upon experience I had gained years earlier in General Motors. I adopted the GM representative system, for example, using GM's manual on dealer management as my guide. And I made a thorough examination of our operations from every aspect: how cars should be sold to ordinary people in contrast to government or business, how financial management for dealers

See p. 117, Col. C, "Spread of Automobile Insurance System."

57

should be run, and so on. To modernize the management of dealer outlets, I requested that strict attention be paid especially to inventory control and to money flows.

We had adopted a fixed-price system by 1952, and in 1953, as we moved to promote a more sophisticated automobile marketing system, we urged our dealers to begin employing college graduates as house salesmen. We subsequently set up training facilities for these salesmen.

In addition, I approved investments in auto-related facilities in hopes of expanding the number of potential customers for automobiles, thereby increasing the possibility of achieving volume car sales. We made investments such as establishing and operating driver training schools, auto mechanic schools, and

Chubu Nippon Automobile School (1957). This school not only taught driving techniques but emphasized road manners and driving safety.

See p. 119, Col. C, "College Graduates Employed as Salesmen" and p. 121, Col. C, "Expansion and Improvement of Toyota's After-sales Service Organization."

58

service centers. Many outsiders thought that we were attempting to diversify, that our investments were wasteful, and that it was unwise to lock funds into non-essential investments when the Company was suffering from a shortage of cash. For instance, our investment in the Chubu Nippon Driving School, opened in 1957, was criticized. We spent ¥400 million to establish this school, and people branded the expenditure as "reckless, something no person in his right mind would do."

However, my aim in establishing this school was to begin creating an environment that would facilitate the spread of motorization. To expand the automobile market, we first had to build a latent demand, without which nothing could be expected in the future. If the number of persons holding driving licenses is small, the demand for automobiles will be small. No one will argue that point. To increase demand, therefore, to increase the number of drivers, we invested in the school. That investment proved worthwhile, incidentally, and when a driving school boom swept the nation around 1960 the Chubu Nippon Driving School became a model for other schools throughout the country. Many people visited our school to observe its operation, which fact alone convinced me that the investment had been a good one.

Our move into the lubricant oils field was also severely criticized, but it also proved to be successful. During my trip to the United States in 1950 I was amazed by the great number of gasoline stations I saw, and by the close relationship that existed between oil companies and companies selling automobiles. Consumption of lubricant oils increases, of course, as more automobiles appear, and I knew therefore that sales of lubricant oils would grow rapidly in Japan as they had done in the United States. When I returned home, I immediately moved to have Toyota enter the lubricant oils business.

We chose Standard Vacuum Oil Company as our partner in this new business, mainly because I had seen firsthand in the

See p. 119, Col. C, "Chubu Nippon Driving School."

United States how Esso- and Mobil-affiliated companies acted with consumer interests in mind. Their marketing approach exactly fit my own approach. Toyota Motor Sales and Standard Vacuum signed a contract in May 1953 and Toyota began selling lubricant oils nationwide under the brand name "Castle," which refers to Nagoya Castle in Toyota's home district. After Standard Vacuum Oil Company was dissolved in late 1961, Toyota completed a contract with Esso Standard Oil Company on April 1, 1962.

Other indispensable parts of our over-all effort to promote motorization were investments in the tourist industry, in industrial film production, in road improvement projects and in an automobile insurance plan. I have always held that just as investments in infrastructures are necessary for production, so also are they necessary for sales. Short-term measures to satisfy present needs seem too often to counter the effect of long-term measures to satisfy future needs. Therefore, instead of concentrating on Toyota's short-term need for cash, as our critics would have had us do, we concentrated on Toyota's long-term need for an environment facilitating volume production.

Some people have called me the "Titan of car sales in Japan," but I have never personally sold a single vehicle. If someone asked me what brought me my limited success, I would say that I have always tried to judge what conditions were needed for automotive sales and to forecast how such conditions could be realized in the future. My sales programs certainly would never have succeeded without the aid of others, particularly our dealers — without their understanding of our programs, and without their cooperation in them.

An important reason for Toyota's success has been its ability to develop its own technology. In 1952 the dominant trend in the Japanese auto industry was to establish technical tie-ups with foreign automakers, tie-ups which usually called for assembling cars in Japan with imported parts and technology, for through such assembly and related tie-ups, auto production technology could be learned. This trend emerged just after Japan and the United States signed the San Francisco Peace Treaty, officially ending the war and returning to Japan its independence. Until then Japanese automakers had been prohibited from producing passenger cars, first by wartime controls and later by Occupation controls.

Controls had been eased somewhat in June 1947 when GHQ issued a memorandum permitting 300 passenger cars to be produced annually, and controls were totally removed in October. But the technical level for passenger car production in Japan then was still far below the level in the United States and Europe. Japanese automakers by 1952 had concluded that the most effective policy for closing this gap quickly was tie-ups with foreign makers. Nissan, Isuzu, Hino and Mitsubishi adopted that policy with quite favorable results.

Toyota, however, after examining the cooperative arrangements for assembly technology from every angle, elected to develop its own technology, although the risks were great. This decision was made for four practical reasons. First, we had confidence in the technical skill of Toyota engineers, for Kiichiro Toyoda had ordered that Toyota continue its research on passenger car development even during the war years when such research was officially banned. Second, we were reluctant to build automobiles using imported parts when we knew that precisely because they contained such parts they could not be exported. Third, we would be frustrated in production activities because we knew that government quotas on the volume of imported automobile parts changed together with changes in the size of the nation's foreign currency reserves. Finally, we would be hampered if unfavorable trends developed toward imports in the over-all policy of the Ministry of International Trade and Industry (MITI).

Our decision could have hurt Toyota Motor Sales Company,

See p. 114, Col. B, "Succession of Foreign Technical Tie-ups."

Toyota Motor Company and Toyota dealers. If we had failed to develop a domestic-made passenger car that could compete with vehicles assembled in Japan with imported parts, Toyota might have been forced to withdraw from the passenger car market. But despite the great risk involved, we turned down every proposal for technical cooperation offered by foreign companies, and our engineering staff began working even harder to raise Toyota's technology level. It took three years from then, three years of dangerous risk, before Toyota produced the Crown, a car capable of competing with all models having foreign parts, and Japan's first purely domestic passenger car.

As President of Toyota Motor Sales Company, I searched for ways in which we in marketing could support production of the Crown. I estimated at the time that if Toyota could reach a monthly production level of 1,000 vehicles, we could compete effectively against foreign models and against domestic models with foreign parts. We took three steps to improve our sales system before introducing the Crown.

One step was to seek the understanding and cooperation of companies in the for-hire and taxi businesses, since about 70 per cent of the demand then for passenger cars came from these companies. If these two groups of companies decided to buy cars assembled using imported parts, Toyota's sales prospects would be dim. I recalled how I had learned in 1935, when we first put a domestic car on the market, that it was unrealistic to expect car sales to improve solely on the basis of patriotic appeal. I knew that true support for the Company would come only if customers bought our products because by doing so they would benefit personally.

The second step we took in the mid-1950s was to lower our retail prices drastically. We lowered prices because we could not wait for costs to drop, and we hoped that lower prices would stimulate demand. Stronger demand would then let us raise production — one way of bringing costs down. That was

See p. 120, Col. B, "Demand for Passenger Cars in Taxi and For-hire Industry" and p. 121, Col. C, "Introduction of Crown and Corona Models."

the pricing policy I backed at the time, and while such a policy does not fit all situations it proved quite effective when we first entered the market. After discussions with President Ishida of Toyota Motor Company, prices for the Toyopet series — the only passenger cars we had in the early 1950s, cars designed with some truck components — were cut by ¥100,000 in August 1952, and by another ¥150,000 in January 1953. We thus sold the Toyopet SF for ¥950,000, which was ¥200,000 less than cars then being built with imported parts. We based our price decisions on the assumption that Toyota Motor Company would produce 500 cars a month. Since the Company was still producing only about 200 cars a month when we lowered prices, however, cost pressures were severe. All we could hope for was success in our aim to stimulate demand. As things turned out, our price-reduction policy was welcomed by the for-hire and taxi companies, and increased sales to them let us survive a period of difficulties.

The third step we took to promote sales was to establish Tokyo Toyopet Company in March 1953, a dealer outlet in Tokyo under the direct management of Toyota Motor Sales Company. Although establishing Tokyo Toyopet under direct management contradicted the principle I hold that dealer outlets should be managed and controlled by local capital, I believed at the time that since Toyota had decided to manufacture passenger cars without depending on foreign technical assistance, it was absolutely necessary to reinforce the passenger car sales system quickly in the Tokyo market. Tokyo accounted for 30 per cent of the nation's entire passenger car market, and the success or failure of Toyota's first wholly domestic-made passenger car depended greatly upon how well it sold in Tokyo. Not only would sales in Tokyo influence sales elsewhere throughout the nation, but imported cars were about to be brought into the Japanese market and we had no time either to bolster existing outlets or to search for capital to

See p. 117, Col. C, "Establishment of Tokyo Toyopet and Its Impact on Tokyo Market."

Head Office Building of Tokyo Toyopet immediately after company's establishment (1953).

establish new outlets.

Other than to bolster our Tokyo sales network, there were at least two additional reasons for establishing Tokyo Toyopet. One was that we wanted to use Tokyo Toyopet for trying out an entirely new sales program. We felt that a more sophisticated sales system was needed in order to increase the social prestige of our operations, and we felt therefore that dealers should employ college graduates as salesmen, promote sales training, implement a standard price system, actively develop strong bases in dealer territories, and improve their service facilities. But if dealers adopted such policies they would naturally have to run great risks. We reasoned, therefore, that if we ourselves conducted experiments through Tokyo Toyopet

See p. 127, Col. C, "Sales Training Organization."

we could better judge the results and then decide whether or not to expand the new sales program nationally. In short, we wanted to avoid forcing unnecessary burdens or risks on our dealers.

The other reason for establishing Tokyo Toyopet under our direct control was that we expected it to serve as a buffer for protecting Toyota Motor Company from having to cut production. One of the three original points in separating Toyota Motor Company and its sales department was that Toyota should not produce more cars than could be sold. But the situation which had developed was much too serious for us to continue this policy for passenger cars. We had to reach a sales level of 1,000 cars per month as soon as possible, the minimum level necessary for competing against imported cars and against domestics with imported parts. If we reduced production merely because of deflated demand in a period of recession, it would delay completion of our passenger car production system. It was imperative to expand Toyota Motor Company's output steadily, even at the risk of over-production, and any surplus would have to be handled by improved sales. While we could not force large inventories on independent dealers, Tokyo Toyopet would be financed with Toyota capital and therefore we could use it as a buffer for unsold cars.

We gained the understanding of our dealers before we set up Tokyo Toyopet under direct control, and setting it up let us maintain our share of the passenger car market. Until we developed the Crown, our passenger cars combined the characteristics of trucks and passenger cars. It would have been impossible to maintain our foothold in the market without making extraordinary efforts to bolster our sales organization, especially the establishment of Tokyo Toyopet.

Just because Tokyo Toyopet was under our direct control did not mean that we rejected the principle that dealers should be capitalized and managed locally. We now have 253 dealers throughout Japan, and — except for some in Tokyo and a few other places under our direct control — all outlets are owned and operated by local people. Moreover, because of the terrific changes that have occurred in the Japanese automobile industry since 1953, the vanguard nature of Tokyo Toyopet and the buffer role it originally played are no longer important considerations.

In 1956 we changed the one-prefecture one-dealer system into a system that gave each prefecture multiple dealers. We did this because we wanted to establish sales channels quickly for the SKB truck (we later renamed it the Toyo-Ace) and a new passenger car, the Corona.

Existing dealers, of course, thought that the new policy of multiple dealers would infringe on their private interests. But I explained to them that if we could increase over-all sales volume and reduce costs, our success would ultimately profit them. In order to expand adequately, I emphasized, we had to increase the number of dealer outlets.

After convincing our dealers, we set up new sales outlets for new models as we marketed them. Besides outlets for the

SKB truck when introduced to market (1954). This truck was the first Toyota product planned and developed on the basis of modern marketing strategy, and it contributed greatly to Toyota's marketing experience.

See p. 119, Col. C, "Introduction of SKB Light Truck" and p. 125, Col. C, "Multiple Marketing Channels."

Toyo-Ace and the Corona, we established the Publica dealer outlet when the Publica was marketed, and the Auto dealer outlet when the Sprinter was marketed. Both of these were passenger cars. In addition, Toyota Motor Company started building new plants to produce new models, for we all thought that if we bolstered only the sales network sales might outpace production, causing an imbalance. For continued efficiency in management we had to strengthen production and sales simultaneously.

The next major development in Toyota's growth, after creating specialized plants and sales outlets, was to meet guidelines proposed by the government for marketing a "people's car."

Let me introduce the "people's car" by mentioning the government's economic white paper published for fiscal year 1956. In it the government wrote that the postwar period was over, that growth tied to recovery from the war was over, and that future growth would be tied to modernization. The government wrote about aiming to make Japan highly industrialized, and thus it put great demands on the automobile industry, one of the most crucial industries for economic expansion.

67

On September 1, 1955, about one year before publication of that white paper, I was appointed an adviser to the Ministry of International Trade and Industry (MITI). My main function was to advise the government concerning the automobile industry. But another important function I had was to assist in preparing details of MITI's proposal for developing a "people's car." The government announced its guidelines for this car in May 1955, outlining vehicle specifications, performance characteristics, retail selling price, and other features. MITI also hinted that government assistance might be given to automakers who produced a vehicle following its guidelines. Automakers, of course, showed an interest in the project, as

See p. 114, Col. A, "The Postwar Period Is Already Over...," p. 116, Col. A, "Period of High Economic Growth" and p. 118, Col. B, "Concept of 'People's Car.' "

did companies in many other industries. Despite studies by various companies, however, Japanese industry was not yet technologically sophisticated enough to follow the guidelines exactly, and the project never materialized.

But Toyota had long dreamed of developing a passenger car for the average Japanese family, and we decided to push ahead with production of a small car that would follow MITI's guidelines as closely as possible. In August 1955 we publicly showed our first prototype of that car in order to demonstrate clearly our willingness to cooperate with the government. But still, like other automakers, Toyota recognized that costs and market conditions were not yet conducive for producing a "people's car," and we were forced to postpone production and sale of that car. Eventually, after undergoing many improvements, the prototype was marketed as the Publica. I knew, of course, that the market for small passenger cars had not yet expanded enough — even though Japan was already experiencing rapid economic growth — but I agreed to introduce the Publica in order to stimulate the market's development. I knew, too, of course, that Toyota would have special difficulties to face as a market pioneer.

While working to develop the small-car market by selling the Publica, I also tried to anticipate ways in which Toyota could take the lead in that market. I met and talked frequently with Taizo Ishida, President of Toyota Motor Company, and we decided to initiate some drastic policy changes. Toyota Motor Company started building a special plant at Motomachi-kita for assembling about 10,000 Publicas a month, and Toyota Motor Sales Company started establishing a special sales network solely for marketing small cars.

After restudying the various methods of selling small cars, I finally decided on widespread adoption of American sales methods, including an open territory system in which a number of dealer outlets would operate in each territory, a cash-on-

See p. 131, Col. C, "Development of Popular Car Market."

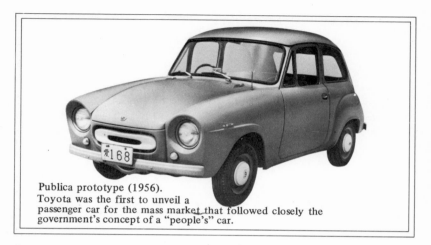

Publica prototype (1956).
Toyota was the first to unveil a
passenger car for the mass market that followed closely the
government's concept of a "people's" car.

delivery system for dealer inventory payments, a customer loan system, and other innovations. But sales failed to grow as rapidly as we had hoped. Although the car we developed was inexpensive and highly efficient, its sales were surprisingly low. We were forced to continue trial-and-error marketing efforts, a process which exhausted me mentally and physically. My health deteriorated so badly that for a while I grew pessimistic about Toyota's whole future. But an era of liberalized trade was coming, and I talked myself into getting better and even began hoping that we could eventually export the Publica. To do so, we started negotiations for a tie-up with Ford Motor Company. Ford had been closely watching the expanding automobile market in Japan, and we, in turn, felt that a tie-up with Ford would help Toyota develop greater export capacity. I wanted to gain a share of the international market for Toyota quickly because of approaching trade liberalization.

Chapter Five

"The World is Our Market"

Toyota's history of negotiations with foreign automakers began when General Motors approached Toyoda Automatic Loom Works in 1936. Restrictions on foreign automakers were about to take effect then, and GM-Japan, whose earlier attempt at an agreement with Nissan Motors had failed, was searching for a Japanese partner. Kiichiro Toyoda was not against foreign investment in the Company, and often said that Toyoda could learn much from such a relationship and that we should continue studying foreign technology. Yet he refused GM's offer of a tie-up. He felt that since Toyoda's automotive activities were still confined as a part of Toyoda Automatic Loom Works, the time was therefore not ripe for the kind of agreement GM had in mind. The negotiations with GM thus stopped almost before they started.

Toyota has negotiated four different times since 1938 with Ford Motor Company. One reason we talked with Ford instead of General Motors when we considered a tie-up was that Ford's policy allowed foreign partners to export completed automobiles back to the United States. Another reason was that the two companies had a basic policy difference in their overseas dealings. GM held that engines and other major auto components could not be made outside the United States, but Ford said the Japanese partner could manufacture such components if it wanted. Since our aim in affiliating with a foreign manufacturer was to acquire technical know-how, I maintained that we could gain more from an arrangement with Ford than with General Motors.

Our first negotiations in 1938 with Ford went very well. By the end of the year we had reached a basic agreement and I was scheduled to visit Ford's offices in Detroit in order to finalize details. Two days before I was to leave Japan, however, the Japanese Army Ministry suddenly ordered Toyota to break off the negotiations. Since we had permission from the Army Ministry's Bureau of Supplies and Equipment to conduct the negotiations, that order was a complete surprise. We were not told the reasons for it but later learned that it had been issued because the Army Ministry's Bureau of Military Affairs in charge of affairs in Manchuria and elsewhere on the Asian continent strongly opposed the ideas of the Bureau of Supplies and Equipment. The first Toyota-Ford negotiations for establishing a business relationship thus failed because of a bureaucratic struggle for control over Japanese industry.

After the two bureaus in the Army Ministry settled their differences we were told that a business tie with Ford would be allowed if Nissan were included in the venture, and talks were started among the three companies. The talks went smoothly and we all agreed to establish a joint-company with an initial capitalization of ¥60 million. Toyota and Nissan would each supply 30 per cent of the capital and Ford would supply 40 per cent. This agreement was made, if I remember right, around the end of 1939. But, again, events turned out badly. Nissan President Ayukawa, the person responsible for that company's part in the talks, suddenly left for Germany, and Masahiro Murakami, acting president in Ayukawa's absence, was uncooperative. He said that since Ayukawa had not left him specific instructions about the negotiations, he could not take responsibility for the agreement. Not long afterward, relations between Japan and the United States turned bad, and the negotiations were stopped completely.

The third round of negotiations with Ford started in June 1950, immediately after the establishment of Toyota Motor Sales Company. There had been a complete cessation of passenger car production in Japan from about 1940, and in order to make up for our resultant lack of technology Kiichiro Toyoda suggested that we consider an agreement with Ford in hopes of gaining know-how for small-car manufacturing. I thought his idea was a good one, and I felt further that we could also expect Ford to aid us in exporting. I took it upon myself to handle the negotiations. Ford was cooperative, and I went to the United States to discuss details. After preliminary discussions in Detroit, Ford agreed to send four of its technicians to Toyota, and even named the four men. This agreement made Kiichiro happy.

For the third time, however, events went badly. On June 25, 1950, the day that I left for the U.S. for talks with Ford, war broke out in Korea. Probably because of the war, the U.S. State Department set emergency restrictions on overseas investments and on the overseas dispatch of technicians. Ford was not allowed to commit itself further, and although we came very close to a formal agreement the negotiations fell through.

In 1960 Toyota and Ford negotiated again, this time in order to market the Publica overseas. As in the three previous negotiations, I was Toyota's representative. Ford wanted a full-scale tie-up but we proposed establishing a joint-venture company, with capital provided at a ratio of 60 per cent from Toyota (40 per cent Toyota Motor Company; 20 per cent Toyota Motor Sales Company) and 40 per cent from Ford. One of our conditions for this joint-venture was cooperation in producing the Publica, which we had already prepared for marketing. Another condition was that when the joint-venture reached a proper stage of development, it should merge with Toyota Motor Company. We asked Ford to study the conditions of our proposal, but negotiations tapered off. Perhaps Ford saw no immediate merit in dealing with us, and it seemed more urgent for them to develop their operations in Europe then. Thus the fifth attempt to negotiate a tie-up with foreign capital ended as unsuccessfully as the previous four attempts.

I was somewhat disappointed with the failure of our talks because I have always felt that in order to gain a solid footing in the domestic automobile market Toyota had to develop a capacity to export as well. Ford put no restrictions on its foreign partners, and I had hoped that we could export to the United States with Ford's help. After the failure of our attempts to negotiate with Ford in 1960, we turned to finance, design, and produce export models completely on our own.

Our interest in exporting related closely to the fact that the automobile is an international commodity and that its use is unrelated to nationality or race. The automotive industry, therefore, must give constant, careful attention to international as well as domestic competition. Toyota's attempts to affiliate with foreign automakers were made out of management necessity, but underlying those attempts was Kiichiro Toyoda's insistence that we learn whatever new technology had to be learned, and my belief that cooperation with foreign capital was useful for our export business. And although Toyota's past talks with foreign companies were not fruitful, this belief remained a major consideration in my management decisions. Kiichiro firmly believed that we could serve the country best by building domestic automobiles that were able to compete successfully with foreign cars in the Japanese market. I wanted to export domestic cars in order to accumulate foreign currency.

In 1949 I was appointed a director in the newly established Association for the Promotion of Automobile Exports. But throughout the 1945-55 period the Japanese auto industry's competitiveness in overseas markets was extremely weak, for none of the domestic auto manufacturers had sufficient financial or production capacity to embark on international

Kamiya at Haneda International Airport prior to second postwar trip to United States (1955).

See p. 116, Col. B, "First Japan Motor Show."

ventures. It was therefore impossible at the time to promote inroads into the international market. In 1955, however, I began seriously thinking of exporting to the United States, the country we considered to be the "home" of the automobile. That year I made my second postwar trip to America, and I gained a strong impression then that popular demand there for automobiles was changing. I noticed especially that there were more small cars on the road. Five years before, I had not seen any small cars in the United States, and I concluded during my second trip that the market for small cars was emerging. I felt that Japan had a chance to enter this new American market, and on the plane from Los Angeles to Washington, D.C., I decided that Toyota should export to America soon. I clearly remember thinking about Japan's economic conditions. At the time, Japanese businessmen had tight restrictions placed on the amount of dollars they could carry out of the country. That and other restrictions were inhibiting Japanese business to such an extent that Japan's economic development was suffering. I felt that acquiring foreign currency was a most important task. Since the American automobile market is so large, we would earn dollars if we could succeed in introducing our cars there; this might be possible, because the market in the U.S. for small cars was just opening. But Toyota did not have a passenger car good enough to compete with American domestics and at first I shrugged off my idea as too fanciful. The thought kept returning, however, and I grew discouraged. I turned my ideas over and over during the flight, and before reaching Washington I regained my confidence and pledged that though exporting was not possible then, we would make it possible in the future.

Immediately after I returned to Tokyo I announced at a Board of Directors meeting that I wanted to start exporting to the United States. The response to my announcement was negative, and I imagined that everyone balked at the idea because of the awesome gap between Japanese and American industrial, technological and competitive capabilities. Everyone at the meeting seemed to think it would be wiser to wait until we could compete better with the American automakers. I sensed beforehand that my colleagues would reject my idea, but I had no intention of rejecting it myself. I gave the group a detailed account of the market in the United States: the changes in the automobile market, the success of European imports, the possibility of future import restrictions and other observations. I finally got them to support my idea. Meanwhile, Toyota Motor Company executives had become quite confident of the Crown, and they felt that an attempt to prepare for the American market would stimulate further improvement of production technology. Therefore, they

Ceremony marking first factory shipment of Crown (1955). This was the first wholly domestic-made passenger car, and Toyota's future rested on its success or failure. Those attending this ceremony wore tuxedos, suggesting the great hope placed in the Crown.

Crown model sample exports to U.S. (1957). The export of passenger cars to the United States was finally to be realized.

supported my proposal.

The time finally came in the spring of 1957 to take concrete steps for exporting to the United States, for the demand there for small cars, which had just only begun two years earlier, had become quite large. European cars had grown so popular that they accounted for about 5 per cent of the whole U.S. market. I felt that even though the United States was the "home" of the automobile, the American government probably could not ignore the increase in imported cars. We worked on the assumption that the American government might eventually place import restrictions on foreign cars and, if it did so, there was a strong possibility that Japanese cars, still never exported successfully, would never get a foothold in the American market. If we really wanted to export cars to the United States there was no time to waste. Regardless of the difficulties, we had to get a foothold that could be strengthened in the future; we needed export results immediately, and later we could work to develop an organization.

August 25, 1957, was a memorable day in Toyota's history: two Crown passenger cars were hoisted aboard ship in Yoko-

77

See p. 127, Col. C, "First Japanese Automaker to Export to U.S."

hama, bound for the United States as samples of our first export product to that country. The export of Japanese cars to the United States was still a conversation piece in the Japanese automobile industry, but Toyota went ahead and took the first step to make into a reality what up to then had been only a hope. Full-scale exports did not start until October, after Toyota Motor Sales, U.S.A., was established, but I will never forget the feeling I had when the first two sample cars sailed from Yokohama on August 25, 1957. I felt almost like I was seeing my children off on a long journey.

But there was much disappointment to follow. We had expected some technical difficulties overseas, but were not prepared to handle the wave of troubles that came. Japanese cars were just not able to meet the performance standards for operating on American highways. After the Crown, in 1960 we exported the Corona (its export name was the Tiara), but it, too, could not compete in the U.S.

I had special reasons for wanting to introduce the Corona to the American market. During a visit to the U.S. in 1958, I became aware of several important trends in the imported car market. The most important one was that the number of small-car imports that year was about 300,000 vehicles. Though this number accounted for only a small percentage of the entire market, if imports continued to grow at the same pace they would reach 10 per cent of the market before long. And while fortunately there were no signs of import restrictions in the U.S., it was still very possible that American automakers themselves would develop a small car just to compete with the imports. To try to counter that possibility, I felt that we should export smaller cars than the Crown in order to avoid direct confrontation with small American-built cars.

My prediction turned out correct. Almost as if they knew each other's plans, the Big Three all introduced compact cars in their 1960 lines. As a result, sales of imported European cars

Los Angeles Imported Automobiles Show (1958).

fell sharply. Toyota also took a beating. Our best marketing strategies failed us, and we were forced to withdraw completely from the market. We had to wait until 1964 to export to the United States again, but we had established Toyota Motor Sales, U.S.A., and we would depend on it for our impetus in 1964.

The press in 1960 gave me credit for having foreseen the appearance of the American compact. More than because of any special talent or perception, however, I think I guessed correctly because I was able to put myself in the position of the Big Three. Experience in business and private life has made me believe that one must be able to view matters from the other person's position, and must respect other opinions. I think an empathetic approach is necessary not merely in business but also in daily life.   Hardly a day passes without something requiring negotiations, and if one stubbornly refuses to reconsider his stand or to understand what others feel or want, then confrontation can only breed more confrontation.   I ask myself what the other party thinks of a matter I am being persistent about, because such a question might provide an idea I might otherwise not have thought of, a clue to the solution of an otherwise difficult problem.   My prediction that the Big Three would fight imports with their own small cars came from my belief that I would have done the same if I had been in their position.

Toyota's response to the American compacts was the Corolla. During my forty years with Toyota, I have introduced many

Crown model change was first in eight years (1962). A lively advertising campaign made the new Crown a subject of popular interest.

Part of Corona "torture" course (1962). The Corona was run over a tough obstacle course to impress strongly on consumers its ruggedness.

new types of automobiles to the market. Each one was special, and each brought me mixed feelings of pleasure and disappointment. Of all those cars, however, I became especially fond of the Corolla. It was the Corolla that most successfully fulfilled our expectations for boosting sales at home and building an export market.

We worked particularly hard to develop the Corolla as a large-volume seller in overseas markets. Our engineers labored from the earliest R&D stages to build a vehicle which would meet all international standards of excellence for the mass market. I personally requested a styling change, and got involved in the design and production stages — something unusual for the head of a sales company.

At a press conference held after the first public showing of the Corolla in late 1966, I expressed confidence that the Corolla would within a short period have a total monthly sales volume, domestic and overseas, of 30,000 cars, thus indicating my high expectations for the model. Toyota's entire production then was about 50,000 units a month, and my statement sounded far too optimistic to many. But such was the confidence I had.

Introduction of Crown RS40 (1962). Toyota felt that this car would compete favorably with imports.

We were in the middle of a business upswing, large wage increases were being given annually, and the public was demanding more from the automobile as consumer purchasing power rose. As it turned out 1966 was the first year in an era of widespread private passenger car ownership, when even the ordinary citizen could have a car.

Toyota's mass-sales network had been developed for handling the Publica, the "car of the public." But now we were putting a fine new automobile, the Corolla, into the sales network. Although Toyota's exports began to grow with the marketing of the Corona RT-40 in 1964, the introduction of the Corolla stimulated a dramatic increase in exports. The number of cars exported in 1964 was 24,000. By December 1968, two years after the Corolla went on the market, we were selling 30,000 units a month. The Corolla joined with the new model Corona, and exports climbed until they reached 280,000 cars in 1968 alone, more than a ten-fold increase in less than five years. Today, together with its sister car, the Sprinter, production of the Corolla series is over 60,000 units a month, making it the world's third top production model after the Beetle and

See p. 132, Col. A, "Structural Recession," p. 131, Col. C, "Reinforcing Export Organization," p. 133, Col. C, "New Corona and Corolla: Success in Mass Production" and p. 139, Col. C, "Toyota's Corolla Becomes World's Top Production Model."

Meeting of Toyota executives for discussing ways to increase exports (1962).

the Chevrolet. The Corolla's success owes much to the great response it has received at home but it has also been received well overseas.

In June 1967 I received the Prime Minister's Award for achievements in developing export trade. That award was especially meaningful to me because it symbolized recognition of the efforts I had put into achieving an ideal. I believed that exporting was a way of acquiring foreign currency and a way of contributing to the growth of the nation, and the Prime Minister's Award meant that my work was appreciated.

Toyota's exports continued to grow rapidly, and Toyota Motor Sales Company became first in Japan's 1970 export ranking. I had badly wanted to start exporting to the United States more than ten years earlier in order to earn Japan more foreign currency but had failed because our products were not suitable for American roads. Who in Toyota could ever have imagined then that one day the Company would be ranked the top exporter in the nation?

After 1970, however, arguments became more pronounced for revaluating the yen upward, and much discussion surfaced

See p. 134, Col. A, "Revaluation of Yen" and p. 139, Col. C, "Toyota Exported Its 5-millionth Vehicle in May 1975."

concerning exporting. Most people felt that exports were now harmful. This trend of argument rose to a fervor about the middle of 1970. By then Japan was no longer a mid-level industrialized nation; as one of the world's top economic powers, it would no longer be wise for Japan to follow the previous policy of emphasizing exports in order to obtain foreign exchange. An export policy based on interdependence and mutual benefits with other advanced countries was becoming increasingly necessary. Those of us who had directly participated in expanding the export market were aware of this necessity, and we began reviewing our concept of exporting long before the need was mentioned by people outside Toyota. Based on our review we began implementing a new international policy.

There was a popular argument for a unilateral easing of exports in 1970, but we felt that the argument ignored certain essential points. Japan has no natural resources, and has no choice except to remain an independent trading nation. It thus seems quite clear that Japan has to export, and I have continued to work toward developing overseas markets. And as we face a period today in which oil prices have skyrocketed, Japan is again threatened by disruptions in its balance of payments. But I feel strongly that the importance of exports must not be evaluated in terms of short-range events.

Another reason for continuing to increase exports in 1970 was that Japan had been pressured to open her doors to foreign car imports and foreign capital, and her industries could only face this new competition by increasing their exports.

The move toward trade liberalization started in the first half of the 1960s. In January 1960, in order to meet changes in the international economic environment, the Japanese government set up a Cabinet Council to Promote Liberalization of Trade and Exchange, and this Council immediately began outlining a plan for trade liberalization. The government was still wary of opening the country widely to foreign competition then, but pressure from the United States and Europe forced liberalization much sooner than we expected. We in the automobile industry felt that we had to raise our international competitive capabilities if we hoped to meet the challenges of liberalization.

Of all industries, the automobile industry was considered the most vulnerable to trade liberalization. Except for trucks, production of vehicles was still relatively small in volume, and our passenger cars were no match for American or European models in quality or price. People outside the industry predicted that Japanese cars would lose the entire market if all restrictions on imported cars were lifted. The country could not afford a decline in its auto industry, which played an essential role in high-growth economic planning and was vital for expanding Japanese exports. Thus the government wanted to delay liberalizing the import of passenger cars as long as possible.

I estimated that the longest we could hold out against overseas pressures would be perhaps three years. In other words, imported passenger cars would be freed from restrictions around the end of 1963. And I felt that we should put more effort into strengthening the industry than into pleading for more time from other countries. We would have to reorganize the whole industry in order to cope with the new competition, and I was responsible for making some very serious administrative decisions and designing a program to help bolster the industry.

In my New Year's Message on January 1, 1960, I asked for support for a new program. I said, in part:

Up to now we have thought only about expanding our exports, and we have kept our own ports closed through foreign exchange restrictions and tariff barriers. But it will no longer be possible to expand into foreign markets unless our own ports are opened to other countries. Since we are reducing our costs by exporting domestic passenger cars to foreign countries, there is no longer any reason to prevent foreign cars from entering Japan. If there is even a slight chance that our cars will be shut out of foreign markets just because our ports are shut to foreign cars, there is no question about how we should proceed if we wish to make profits instead of losses. The industry's wish to postpone removal of trade barriers will only isolate Japan from the rest of the world.

Those words expressed my feeling that we had to cope directly, not passively, with the trend toward liberalization. But while there was a growing body of opinion in Japan that supported liberalization, my program still received much criticism.

People in various fields were dubious; they said that we should not talk about liberalization in that way unless we really were capable of competing. But since I was convinced, as I am today, that good relations with other countries are absolutely vital for promoting exports, and that a spirit of give-and-take is vital for trade harmony, I emphasized the need to strengthen our corporation rather than to postpone liberalization. Toyota introduced a slogan, "Looking Forward to Liberalization," in order to express its positive approach.

Toyota Motor Company worked to set up a monthly production schedule of 30,000 cars while Toyota Motor Sales Company worked to complete a sales system that could sell the same number. Toyota's Motomachi Plant, Japan's first plant built exclusively for passenger car assembly, was running at full capacity, and a new plant was begun in Motomachi-kita. At Toyota Motor Sales Company we worked to strengthen our domestic and overseas sales networks, and by raising more funds we expanded sales, which helped to reduce costs. Toyota first attained a monthly production of 30,000 cars in December

See p. 129, Col. C, "Toward Production of 30,000 Vehicles Monthly."

1963.

By October 1965 restrictions on completely assembled passenger car imports were lifted, although liberalization officially began the previous year together with introduction of the system of automatic government approval of imports. Tariff barriers remained, however, and since the industry's efforts had produced a significant reduction in production costs and a significant improvement in quality, the number of foreign cars sold in Japan was lower than we had expected.

But we could not afford to feel satisfied. We had to make a firm decision on how to deal with capital liberalization. Trade liberalization could be met with better quality and lower costs, but capital liberalization required both of these plus a qualitative strengthening of the corporate and industrial structure. Next, therefore, we had to face the problem of how to reorganize the entire automobile industry through individual corporate cooperation and through government policy.

See p. 134, Col. B, "Lively Discussions about Capital Liberalization."

Chapter Six

The Automobile Industry Grows

The reorganization of the auto industry proceeded slowly before 1965, although there was much talk about how industrial reorganization would be an effective way to cope with trade and capital liberalization. In May 1961 the Ministry of International Trade and Industry (MITI) announced a proposal to have automobile manufacturers merge into three large groups that it believed would make the industry a more effective force in international competition.

After MITI's announcement, discussions about industrial reorganization grew more intense, but all of them occurred outside the automobile industry itself. The rationale behind the proposal for realignment of the auto industry — that by merging the automobile companies, or by creating affiliations among

See p. 130, Col. B, "MITI Concept of Three Company Groups for Producing Passenger Cars."

them, the scale of mass production would be enhanced, which would in turn lead to greater international competitiveness — was thoroughly understood by the industry, but individual companies felt little incentive to carry out the plan because none wanted to discard their individual market aspirations. Moreover, none felt any particular urgency about the threat of either trade or capital liberalization.

But the 1965 recession produced a drastic change in their thinking. The rate of increase in demand for automobiles dropped, and the large investments in plants and equipment that automakers had been making suddenly became a great burden. Furthermore, the belief that the 1965 recession was structural in nature seemed to have affected management thinking in subtle ways, even as the timetable for liberalization was being discussed and it seemed that specific dates might be announced soon.

I had no intention of actively promoting the reorganization of the auto industry, mainly because I was convinced that Toyota Motor Company, Toyota Motor Sales Company and our dealers had all been working hard to strengthen our international competitiveness. At the same time, however, I felt that if the government strongly requested Toyota participation in reorganization, and if our participation would help to create a qualitative improvement in the industry, then we should eagerly cooperate. In other words, I felt that our decisions should not be based on a desire merely to expand the company, but also on national priorities.

The first reorganization of Japan's auto industry took place between 1966 and 1968, and led to business affiliations among the two main Toyota companies, the Hino Motor and Hino Motor Sales Companies, and Daihatsu Kogyo Company. Before we reached a final decision on those ties I personally studied them carefully because of their potential effect on sales.

Company mergers or affiliations involve coordinations, ad-

See p. 135, Col. C, "Toyota's Business Ties with Hino Motors and Daihatsu Kogyo" and p. 136, Col. B, "Moves to Restructure Automobile Industry."

After completing tie-up with Hino Motors, Toyota completed separate tie-up with Daihatsu Kogyo (1967).

justments and the elimination of duplication at various levels. At the production level, for instance, overlapping investments must be avoided by coordinating car models, by ensuring commonality of parts and by cooperating in research and development. Such measures involve many difficult procedural and technical problems, but almost all of them can be handled at the production level, and they are only problems for manufacturers. At the sales level, however, unnecessary burdens on the consumer and on dealers must be avoided. Organizational changes can hurt sales activities seriously.

Our dealers were thus very concerned about my thinking on reorganization. In January 1965, when the appeals for reorganization were strongest, Noboru Yamaguchi, chairman of the Toyota Motor Sales Dealers Association, conveyed to me the unanimous opinion of our dealers. He said they realized that reorganization of the automobile industry was inevitable, and that they would cooperate completely if Toyota Motor Company and Toyota Motor Sales Company decided to follow the government's policy. They understood that there could be considerable benefits in new affiliations, but they hoped that Toyota would consider more than just its own material and manpower benefits. They wanted me to consider carefully how any affiliation would affect their customers and sales. I told them that I understood their position perfectly and that I would handle matters as best I could. They were aware of my strong feeling about the need for mutual understanding.

As it turned out, Toyota's new affiliations did not disrupt sales activities, and the over-all reorganization of the auto industry gave Toyota added strength to cope with the challenges of capital liberalization.

In 1968, American demands that Japan lift its controls on foreign capital investments in the automobile industry grew strong. They continued throughout eight months of automobile negotiations that year between the two countries. The United States was suffering from a decline in the value and prestige of the dollar at the time, and the American government was working through the OECD and GATT to have the Japanese government lift its controls. Pressures to liberalize foreign capital investments in the automobile industry grew because Japan continued to hold off the import of foreign capital in order to protect the domestic industry even as Japanese automakers were increasing their exports to the United States.

American pressure for the early liberalization of foreign investments in the industry remained strong, and gradually even Japanese government leaders and influential persons in the Federation of Economic Organizations (Keidanren) turned in

See p. 132, Col. B, "Japan-U.S. Automobile Negotiations," p. 138, Col. B, "Isuzu Motors Announces Tie-up with General Motors" and p. 138, Col. B, "Mitsubishi Heavy Industries Announces Tie-up with Chrysler Corporation."

favor of it. The Japanese government knew the exact position of the automobile industry, largely because of the efforts of Katsuji Kawamata, then president of the Japan Automobile Manufacturers Association (JAMA), but once the matter had become a political issue between Japan and the United States it became too late to check the trend toward liberalization.

It was obviously impossible to continue our one-sided attempt to justify Japan's position, and it seemed clear, in view of mounting international pressures, that Japan's counter-proposal to lift capital controls after fiscal 1972 was not feasible. Since capital liberalization would probably come sooner rather than later, I proposed that Toyota complete its preparations by the end of fiscal 1970.

On November 3, 1968, I was awarded the Second Order of Merit of the Rising Sun, a government award for my efforts in developing Japan through the promotion of exports. A few days after the award I was asked to speak in Nagoya on the subject of the automobile and liberalization. On that occasion I said that Toyota expected to complete its preparations for capital liberalization by the end of fiscal 1970. Unfortunately, the press reported that I had spoken "strongly in support of early liberalization," which was untrue and which gave the impression that I was causing wide confusion within the industry. In my speech I did not even imply support for an early lifting of controls, and I would have been grateful if even a day's delay had been possible. My real point was that for many reasons delay was not possible and that therefore management in the auto industry had to be ready for liberalization whenever it came.

Around the same time, a similar misunderstanding occurred at a press conference. "It is no longer practical," I said then, "to keep stubbornly refusing to accept every proposal sent our way. We should think instead of how to avoid complete liberalization. We could allow knock-down production of cars over 3,000cc, for example, cars which do not compete directly with our products." As before, the press took my comment to mean that I advocated early liberalization.

Actually, my comments on both those occasions expressed my long-held belief that you must look at things from the other man's viewpoint; you must know what he wants and what he thinks. I had no other motives for my comments.

The liberalization process thereafter turned to our disadvantage at a dismaying pace. Until the fall of 1969 no one thought that liberalization would take place before fiscal 1972, but in October 1969 it was up-dated to October 1971. Ultimately it was speeded up further, with conditions, to April 1971. My proposal that Toyota complete preparations by the end of fiscal 1970 proved to be correct.

If Toyota could produce and sell two million cars a year, we would probably be able to face competition from foreign automakers who invested in Japan. We had to act quickly though, and we proceeded to expand and strengthen our domestic and overseas sales systems, the main instruments of our countermeasures. Our entire organization worked

Toyota's Corolla becomes world's top production model (1974).

See p. 137, Col. C, "Annual Production of One Million, and Then Two Million Vehicles."

together on this project, and we were able to complete most of the system by the 1970 target date. In 1971 our sales were 1,950,000 vehicles, which meant that our goal of two million vehicles was near.

But in order to realize new progress in international business and sales I felt we needed a complete qualitative and quantitative overhaul of our operations, both within the company and among our distributors. Moreover, there were other developments besides capital liberalization that we needed to adapt to, including an emerging concept of corporate social responsibility and other changes affecting the auto industry.

In June 1972, the University of Utah in Salt Lake City, awarded me an honorary doctor's degree in the humanities for

Honorary doctor's degree conferred on Kamiya by University of Utah (1972).

my contributions toward mutual understanding between Japan and the United States. I was granted the award as president of the Nagoya Broadcasting Company, which sponsors a program for sending students living within its service area to the University of Utah for study. The program's aims are to help develop the local community and to recycle corporate profits for public welfare uses. I have always been personally interested in promoting the education of children, for my own experience has impressed on me the important influence that education has on a person's entire life.

On November 3, 1973, moreover, I was awarded the First Order of Merit and the Order of the Sacred Treasure, Japanese government awards that were unexpected and truly high honors

Kamiya receives First Order of Merit and Order of Sacred Treasure (celebration reception, 1973).

for me. I have never intentionally conducted my professional affairs in order to win such lofty recognition, but I knew that those awards came from impartial judges and I accepted them gratefully. The First Order of Merit was for my work in broadcasting, in education, and in securing energy resources, as well as for my work in the automobile industry. But I cannot possibly claim the entire credit for these accomplishments; they resulted from the cooperation of many people, and the awards I received I thus accepted on behalf of them and with heartfelt appreciation.

Our country was put in a difficult situation by the oil embargo. Because of the direct relationship between oil and the automobile, the adverse effect of oil shortages on the auto industry were particularly severe. Yet bad times are perhaps inevitable. At the same time, I believe firmly that good times always follow, not because I have great optimism but simply because of my personal experience in overcoming many difficulties.

Of the original executives of Toyota Motor Company, I am the only one left. In all honesty, Toyota means much to me. The work of helping Toyota grow and of helping Toyota's people realize their ambitions has for me been a kind of mission. Yet I also realize that a corporation is just one part of society, that Japan is just one society in the world, and that the pursuit of only Toyota's interests would be folly. The policies of a corporation must conform not only to the interests of Japan, but also to the needs of every society, however great or small. This thought occupies my mind even during the busiest of days.

"To shoulder a heavy burden down a long road — such is life." For a person like myself who envisages life as a never-ending struggle within the limits of human possibility, these words of the first Tokugawa Shogun, words which I have remembered from early childhood, are forever meaningful and forever inspiring.

See p. 138, Col. B, "Automobile Industry Grows Tremendously."

APPENDIX

These appendices have been prepared
to provide the reader with background
information to Mr. Kamiya's story.

1890

1900

Sino-Japanese and Russo-Japanese Wars, and Japan's Industrialization

Japan fought wars with China in 1894-95 and Russia in 1904-05 over control of Manchuria and Korea. In world history, the Russo-Japanese War marked the advent of a period of imperialism. That war was especially significant in Japanese history because it provided imperialists the opportunity to establish themselves firmly here. Industrialization proceeded rapidly in Japan around the turn of the century, stimulated by growth in military-related industries.

The state-run Yawata Iron and Steel Works (today's Nippon Steel Corporation) began operating in February 1901, and Japanese industry gradually moved from emphasis on light industries centering on textiles to emphasis on the heavy and chemical industries. In particular, the outbreak of World War I in 1914 greatly stimulated industry, and Japan began turning from an agricultural into an industrial nation. During 1914-18 the industrial labor force doubled and the total value of production in real terms more than doubled. The metals, machinery and chemical industries grew particularly fast.

In reaction to the prosperous war years, however, a recession struck Japan in the post-World War I period. Many plants cut production, closed down temporarily or went out of business. The Great Depression of 1929 also affected Japan seriously, and industry experienced especially hard times. Various adjustments in industry had to be made, on the one hand, while production activities became more concentrated, on the other, and production capital tended toward monopolization.

Automatic loom invented by Sakichi Toyoda.

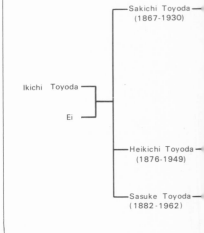

Sakichi Toyoda (1867-1930)

Ikichi Toyoda

Ei

Heikichi Toyoda (1876-1949)

Sasuke Toyoda (1882-1962)

July 9, 1898
Born in Aichi Prefecture.

Sakichi Toyoda (1867-1930)

Sakichi Toyoda is a well-known Japanese inventor, and his life is even outlined in primary school textbooks. As a boy he worked with his carpenter father, but from the age of eighteen he became seriously interested in inventing. He applied for his first patent in 1890, and in 1897 invented the first Japanese power-driven loom, the Toyoda Power-Driven Wooden Loom. He continued to work on looms and in 1926 perfected an automatic loom. He had acquired domestic and overseas patents during this period, and in 1929 he sold the right to use his patents in certain regions to the Blatt Brothers, the world's largest manufacturers then of spinning and weaving machinery. He received 10,000 British pounds from this contract and applied the money to cover Kiichiro's automobile research expenses. Thus, the money that supported Toyoda's first efforts in automobile research and development derived from the sale of patent rights to an automatic loom. Sakichi and his eldest son, Kiichiro, had differing interests — the father in automatic looms and the son in automobiles — but they both were avid inventors.

Mar. 1917
Graduated from Nagoya Commercial High School.

Apr. 1917
Joined Mitsui & Co., Ltd., in Tokyo. Assigned to Seattle in 1918, to London in 1919, and back to Tokyo in 1924.

Toyoda Family Geneology

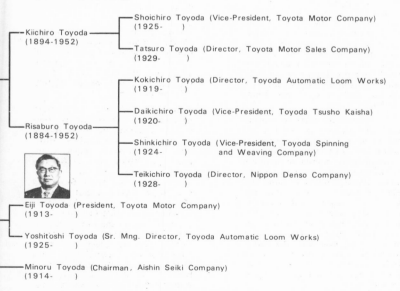

Kiichiro Toyoda
(1894-1952)

- Shoichiro Toyoda (Vice-President, Toyota Motor Company)
  (1925-   )
- Tatsuro Toyoda (Director, Toyota Motor Sales Company)
  (1929-   )

Risaburo Toyoda
(1884-1952)

- Kokichiro Toyoda (Director, Toyoda Automatic Loom Works)
  (1919-   )
- Daikichiro Toyoda (Vice-President, Toyoda Tsusho Kaisha)
  (1920-   )
- Shinkichiro Toyoda (Vice-President, Toyoda Spinning
  (1924-   )   and Weaving Company)
- Teikichiro Toyoda (Director, Nippon Denso Company)
  (1928-   )

Eiji Toyoda (President, Toyota Motor Company)
(1913-   )

Yoshitoshi Toyoda (Sr. Mng. Director, Toyoda Automatic Loom Works)
(1925-   )

Minoru Toyoda (Chairman, Aishin Seiki Company)
(1914-   )

Note: This geneology is valid as of September 1, 1976, and includes only Toyoda family
      members in director or higher posts.

1920

A. Socio-economic Background

Great Kanto Earthquake

At 11:58 a.m. on September 1, 1923, an earthquake of magnitude 7.9 struck the southern Kanto Region, which includes Tokyo and Yokohama. Fires and riots occurred in the earthquake's aftermath, completely destroying over 440,000 homes and leaving 140,000 persons either dead or missing. This was the Great Kanto Earthquake.

Earthquakes are not unusual in Japan, but the Great Kanto Earthquake was especially large. September 1 is now an official Earthquake Memorial Day, and the Japanese populace is kept constantly aware of the possibility of another destructive earthquake. Japanese today recall the Great Kanto Earthquake even when the ground shakes only slightly.

The destruction from the Great Kanto Earthquake bore socio-economic consequences that affected the country's growth. Losses from the earthquake totalled ¥6.5 billion (in 1923 terms), an amount so large that it threw the economy into chaos and caused a depression. The economy had already been suffering from the poor business conditions that followed the end of World War I and the recession of 1922, and the Great Kanto Earthquake thus shook the economy's already severely weakened foundations.

The government declared martial law right after the earthquake and moved to restore public order. It prohibited profiteering activities, introduced a thirty-day banking moratorium and issued earthquake damage notes through the Bank of Japan. In particular, the Bank of Japan rediscounted promissory and other notes that could not be paid because of earthquake losses. The value of these notes, however, reached a tremendous figure by the end of 1923 and caused the amount of bank notes in circulation to expand greatly.

Conditions in Japan worsened steadily, and all the economic contradictions up to then finally emerged in the Financial Panic of 1927.

B. Automobile Industry

Start of Japan's Motorization

Japan's motorization began in the latter half of the 1920s when American-made vehicles were first imported. Only in 1928, however, did the number of motor vehicles in Japan first exceed the number of rickshaws.

Ford-Japan and GM-Japan

Ford-Japan, founded in 1925 and capitalized at 4 million yen, built a plant in Yokohama in 1927 on 37,178m² of land. This plant, which had floor space of 13,966 m², became a base for Ford's operations in Asia. Assembly capacity at the plant was about 7,000-8,000 vehicles per year. In 1929, in preparation for expected growth, Ford-Japan recapitalized to 8 million yen.

GM-Japan, founded in 1927 and capitalized at 8 million yen, began building a plant in Osaka in 1926 on 49,718m² of land. Floor space was 15,668m², and assembly capacity was about 10,000 vehicles per year.

Ford and GM both established national sales and service networks in Japan. Ford, for example, had 80 dealer outlets. Both also established financing companies in 1929, and 70-80 per cent of their sales were credit sales. These moves by Ford and GM hurt Japanese automakers. Hakuyosha, a Japanese automaker established in 1921 (1 million yen capital), was pushed into dissolution. Three other automakers — Tokyo Gas & Electric, Tokyo Ishikawajima Shipbuilding, and Datto Motor Company — were barely saved from bankruptcy by a demand for military-use trucks. But the total production of these three companies remained far below the production of either Ford or GM.

C. Toyota

Toyoda Automatic Loom Works, Ltd.

Toyoda Spinning & Weaving Co., Ltd., established in 1918, grew out of Toyoda Automatic Woven Garments, a company Sakichi Toyoda founded to produce the high quality threads needed to perfect his automatic loom. In 1926, after development of the automatic loom, the loom production department was made independent as Toyoda Automatic Loom Works, Co., Ltd., in order to concentrate on production of automatic looms. Toyoda Automatic Loom Works continues today to manufacture textile machinery, but it also produces Toyota forklifts and small-size commercial vehicles. As of March 31, 1975, the company's capitalization was ¥4,155 million, it had 5,896 employees and its annual sales were ¥112 billion.

D. Kamiya

Sep. 1924
Resigned from Mitsui & Co.

Apr. 1925
Returned to London and established the Kamiya Trading Company as an iron and steel wholesaler.

May. 1927
Closed down Kamiya Trading Company and returned to Japan.

Jan. 1928
Joined General Motors-Japan.

Mix and Volume of Transport Vehicles in Japan: 1908-30   Unit:vehicles

	Passenger cars (incl. buses)	Trucks	All motor vehicles	Rickshaws	Bicycles	Carts	Ox/horse wagons
1908	—	—	9	—	—	—	—
1909	—	—	19	—	—	—	—
1910	—	—	121	—	—	—	—
1911	—	—	235	—	—	—	—
1912	—	—	512	—	—	—	—
1913	—	—	892	—	—	—	—
1914	—	—	1,066	—	—	—	—
1915	—	—	1,244	—	—	—	—
1916	1,624	24	1,648	—	—	—	—
1917	2,647	25	2,672	—	—	—	—
1918	4,491	42	4,533	—	—	—	—
1919	6,847	204	7,051	—	—	—	—
1920	9,355	644	9,999	—	—	—	—
1921	11,228	888	12,116	—	—	—	—
1922	13,483	1,383	14,866	—	—	—	—
1923	10,666	2,099	12,765	—	—	—	—
1924	17,939	6,394	24,333	105,700	3,690,000	1,923,500	374,200
1925	21,002	8,162	29,164	82,900	4,142,200	1,977,800	382,000
1926	27,973	12,097	40,353	72,300	4,597,000	1,963,100	392,400
1927	35,775	15,987	52,102	69,300	4,844,100	1,917,800	403,100
1928	44,660	21,719	66,777	59,200	5,111,700	1,894,100	405,900
1929	52,829	27,541	80,826	50,100	5,602,000	1,812,500	463,300
1930	57,827	30,881	88,708	42,600	5,779,300	1,807,800	407,600

Sources: Annual Statistics, Police and Security Department; Ministry of the Interior

A. Socio-economic Background

Heavy Inflow of Foreign Capital

The flow into Japan of foreign capital was especially great during two periods: 1905-13, between the Russo-Japanese War and the start of World War I; and 1921-26, between the end of World War I and recovery from the devastation of the Great Kanto Earthquake of 1923. The average inflow of capital was ¥180 million annually (approximately 50 per cent of the average balance then of outstanding bank notes) in the first period, and ¥200 million annually (13 per cent of the average balance) in the second period. These were tremendous amounts of money.

About 80 per cent of the incoming capital was from bond flotations abroad, mostly government

B. Automobile Industry

bonds. And while investments in stock for managerial participation in Japan were small, the over-all capital inflow contributed importantly to modernizing Japanese industry.

Some of the firms established with foreign capital in these two periods and still operating in Japan today are Shell Sekiyu (established 1900; The Shell Petroleum Co.); Nippon Light Metal Co., Ltd. (1914; Alcan Aluminum Ltd.); Sumitomo Rubber Industries (1917; Dunlop Rubber Co., Ltd.); Yokohama Rubber Co., Ltd. (1917; The B.F. Goodrich Co.); Japan NCR (1920; The National Cash Register Co.); Toyo Aluminum Ltd.); and Mitsubishi Oil Co., Ltd. (1913; Getty Oil Co.).

Economic Chaos Prior to Great Depression

In 1925, Takada & Co., one of Japan's largest trading firms, went bankrupt after running into business difficulties and being denied financial assistance by the Treasury Ministry. It left debts totalling ¥100 million. This bankruptcy is considered the first indication of serious financial difficulties which culminated in the Financial Panic of 1927. Japan's economic prosperity from 1925 onward declined, and many large companies went bankrupt as financial conditions worsened. In January 1927, there was a deposit

run on the Watanabe Bank, then one of Japan's leading banks. Its business operations had worsened because of mismanagement, and rumors had spread that it suffered heavy losses in the handling of notes that had been issued to stimulate recovery from the Great Kanto Earthquake of 1923. The Watanabe Bank and thirty-six other banks either went bankrupt or closed down temporarily. In April 1927, the Bank of Taiwan suspended its operations, and Suzuki Shoten collapsed.

Japanese Society after Mid-1920s

Sweeping changes began to occur in Japanese society after the Great Kanto Earthquake, particularly in Tokyo and its surrounding region. Changes became especially apparent around 1928. The downtown area of Tokyo, for example, where people had maintained a strongly traditional way of life, was totally destroyed by the earthquake, and inexpensive Western-style housing was built in the area in the years thereafter. Around this same time, modern office buildings were built in Tokyo's Marunouchi business district. Also in the second half of the 1920s, automobiles began

appearing in Japan's cities in greater number, people went to see moving pictures, and life was being enjoyed in popular cafes. It was a period of mass consumption and popular amusement, as well as an age of mass production and mass advertising. But while the economy temporarily recovered a degree of stability, the country still lagged behind the Western countries in the competition for world trade. Meanwhile, the Act for Maintaining Public Security was strengthened, causing restrictions on political activities. Great uncertainty about the future spread among the populace.

C. Toyota   **D. Kamiya**

Motor Vehicles Supplied in Japan: 1925-33   Unit: vehicles

	Domestic-made	CBU imports	KD imports	Total	Breakdown of KD imports	Ford-Japan	GM-Japan	Kyoritsu Motors
1925	376	1,765	3,437	5,578		3,437		
1926	245	2,381	8,677	11,303		8,677		
1927	302	3,895	12,668	16,865		7,033	5,635	
1928	347	7,883	24,341	32,571		8,850	15,491	
1929	437	5,018	29,338	34,793		10,674	15,745	1,251
1930	458	2,591	19,678	22,727		10,620	8,049	1,015
1931	436 (2)	1,887	20,199	22,522		11,505	7,478	1,201
1932	880 (184)	997	14,087	15,964		7,448	5,893	760
1933	1,681 (626)	491	15,082	17,254		8,106	5,942	998

Sources: Industrial Affairs Bureau, Ministry of Commerce and Industry; others
Notes: 1. Figures in parentheses are number of small cars.
2. Total number of KD imports and total of breakdown for KD imports differ but follow the statistics on record.

1930

A. Socio-economic Background

Manchurian and Shanghai Incidents

In September 1931, fighting erupted in Manchuria between Japanese and Chinese troops, thereby providing a reason for the Japanese military to enter Manchuria. This incident — the Manchurian Incident — coupled with the Shanghai Incident of 1932, were the two direct causes for Japan's intervention in China. And as Japan's military actions spread they led to war between China and Japan and continued into World War II. Military-related industries in Japan expanded rapidly and military expenditures grew tremendously. Stimulated by military spending, moreover, military-related technology was modernized, especially in the shipbuilding and aircraft industries. Other industries that prospered included the metals and chemical industries. But Japan's low wage structure, and wage cuts that Japanese industry introduced, brought much criticism from abroad. Countries of the West began taking retaliatory steps such as applying high tariffs against Japanese imports and introducing import controls, and boycott movements of Japanese goods began in many countries.

February 26th Incident

On February 26, 1936, a group of young extremist army officers, calling for reforms in the domestic political structure, led attacks on the official residences of the Prime Minister and the Finance Minister, and on a number of other government offices in Tokyo. They killed the Minister of the Interior and other officials and occupied the area around the National Diet for four days. Although the government suppressed this coup attempt, the military's voice in politics and economics subsequently became much more powerful. This incident greatly stimulated the emergence of the military clique.

B. Automobile Industry

Committee for Establishment of Automobile Industry

Official help in developing the domestic motor vehicle industry began in 1918 with enactment of the Law for Assistance Concerning Military-Use Vehicles. Under this law, the government provided subsidies to automakers in the areas of manufacture, sales and maintenance in return for a promise that the automakers comply in meeting military requirements in an emergency situation. This law proved insufficient by itself to help the automakers.

Moreover, after Ford and GM began operating their new plants the volume of auto-related imports rose rapidly and Japan's balance of international payments worsened considerably. Thereafter, the promotion of the domestic motor vehicle industry became an important item in government policy. In 1931 the Ministry of Commerce and Industry created the Committee for the Establishment of the Automobile Industry in order to study the problems involved in establishing firmly the domestic motor vehicle industry. This committee subsequently formulated standards for domestic-made vehicles and submitted a report that discussed matters such as government protection of and subsidies for the domestic industry. In 1933 the Ministry of Commerce and Industry announced standards for five types of vehicles: 1.5- and 2.0-ton trucks, and 16-, 21- and 25-passenger buses. All five vehicles would use water-cooled, 45hp/1500rpm, 6-cylinder engines. In 1934 Japanese automakers produced 150 vehicles according to these standards.

Government subsidies for FY1934 totaled 75,000 yen.

Into Automobile Industry

In 1933 an Automotive Department was established inside Toyoda Automatic Loom Works, and motor vehicle manufacturing officially became part of the company's business. Up to then, Kiichiro Toyoda had conducted independent research on motor vehicles. He had begun work in 1930 on a prototype engine for a small-size vehicle, and establishment of the Automotive Department reaffirmed his determination to enter the passenger car field. Three general points characterized his thinking regarding the type of vehicle he wanted to produce.

1. He believed that there was no need to avoid competition with Ford and Chevrolet and that a popular car could be produced in volume that combined the best Ford and Chevrolet features, together with other features that met the particular requirements of Japanese customers, while still competing with foreign models in price and performance.
2. He wanted to develop a method of production based on the American system of mass production but adapted to the Japanese situation. It should result from a spirit of research and creativity in design and production methods.
3. He believed that Toyoda had to manufacture on its own as great a percentage of the complete vehicle as possible because of basic weaknesses in Japan's industrial structure which made it impossible to rely on other industries to support automobile manufacturing. For example, the company should have its own facilities for producing components, for making special steels, and for manufacturing production machinery.

Toyoda's plans to manufacture passenger cars caught the interest of the Japanese government, and influenced eventual passage of the Law Concerning the Manufacture of Motor Vehicles.

Toyota finished a prototype passenger car, the Model A-1, in May 1935. But in order to comply with the government's policy then of promoting the production of trucks, Toyota halted production of the Model A-1 after building only three vehicles and concentrated instead on producing trucks.

Oct. 1935
Resigned from General Motors. Joined Toyoda Automatic Loom Works as Sales Manager in the Automotive Department.

107

Law Concerning Manufacture of Motor Vehicles

After the Manchurian Incident of September 1931 the government took a more direct interest in establishing firmly the domestic motor vehicle industry. Some subsidies were already being granted under the 1918 Law for Assistance Concerning Military-Use Vehicles, but now the government urged automakers to work closely together, suggested that the Mitsui, Mitsubishi and other zaibatsu groups enter the automobile industry, and moved to raise substantially the tariff on auto-related imports.

Ford and GM coped with these moves by strengthening their Japanese operations and making their control of the local market more secure. Their plans included complete local manufacture of components and full assembly operations in Japan.

These plans by Ford and GM

made the government recognize more clearly the urgent need for strengthening the domestic motor vehicle industry, and in 1936 it clarified its thinking by enacting the Law Concerning the Manufacture of Motor Vehicles. This law provided in part that automakers would be exempt from income and business taxes for five years, and exempt from duties on materials, tools, machinery and other imported items needed for conducting their manufacturing operations. The law also provided that if necessary the government could order changes in price or in other conditions for the sale of motor vehicles or their components, could order automakers to expand or improve their plants and facilities, and could order other actions for adjusting the supply/demand situation for motor vehicles or their components.

Automobile Industry and Wartime Preparations

Ford-Japan and GM-Japan saw their operations come under severe restrictions as a result of government moves to protect and develop the domestic motor vehicle industry. In 1936, for example, the Ministry of Commerce and Industry restricted Ford's and GM's annual production to, respectively, 12,360 vehicles or less and 9,470 vehicles or less. Import tariffs were revised upward, moreover, and the rate for complete vehicles rose from 50 per cent to 70 per cent (in an agreement with France, from 35 per cent to 49 per cent), for engines it rose from 35 per cent to 60 per cent, and for components it rose greatly in detailed categories.

In 1937, following the outbreak of the China Incident, Japan entered into a semi-wartime situation. The government revised the foreign exchange control law,

and adopted emergency measures toward auto-related imports, moves which resulted in very severe restrictions on the import of complete and knocked-down vehicles. Also, since the Japanese yen dropped in value on world money markets following the China Incident, the price of imports rose tremendously. Ford and GM were hurt by this combination of factors and were forced to halt their production operations beginning in 1939.

In these general circumstances the production of motor vehicles by domestic automakers rose steadily, supported by demand from the military sector. However, demand from the private sector shrank. Beginning in 1938, restrictions were placed on the manufacture of passenger cars, and production of small-size passenger cars was completely halted.

C. Toyota

Toyoda's First Marketed Motor Vehicle, Model G-1 Truck

In August 1935 Toyoda completed the prototype of its first truck, the Model G-1 truck. This truck was shown to the public in November 1935 as Toyoda's first motor vehicle on the market. It had oil brakes, a free-suspension rear axle, a reinforced frame, and other new structural innovations. By the end of 1935 Toyoda produced eighteen of these trucks and sold fourteen. The truck's ex-factory price was 2,900 yen. For comparison, the average monthly salary in 1935 was 30-50 yen for a factory worker and 40-60 yen for an office worker.

Specifications of Model G-1 Truck

Engine . . . . Type A
Length . . . . 5,950 mm
Width . . . . 2,191 mm
Height . . . . 2,219 mm
Wheel Base . . . . . . 3,594 mm
Weight . . . . 2,470 kg
No. of Passengers . . . 2
Max. wt. carried . . . 1,500 kg

"Toyoda" Becomes "Toyota"

In July 1936 Toyoda Automatic Loom Works announced a national contest for a corporate logo design, aiming at the same time to stimulate interest in its Toyoda AA sedan. The design had to have a "speedy" feeling, had to suggest the fact of being a domestic corporation, and had to contain the Japanese syllables トヨダ (TOYODA). While judging the 27,000 entries it was decided that "Toyota" not only sounded clearer than "Toyoda" but also seemed better in terms of advertising psychology. "Toyoda" thus became "Toyota," and "Toyota" was made the product's name beginning in October 1936. The Toyota trademark was registered in April 1937.

Establishment of Toyota Motor Company

In September 1936 Toyoda Automatic Loom Works was officially designated under the Law Concerning the Manufacture of Motor Vehicles as a company allowed to manufacture motor vehicles. By being thus designated, Toyoda became obliged to prepare quickly a production system for manufacturing 3,000 vehicles a year. In 1937 the company began construction of a plant with a combined production capacity of 1,500 trucks and passenger cars a month. The estimated cost of the new plant was ¥30 million. Although Toyoda Automatic Loom Works was prospering then its capitalization was only ¥6 million and the cost of the new plant would surpass its fund-raising capabilities. Thus the idea emerged of making the company's Automotive Department an independent entity. Toyota Motor Company was established in August 1937 with capitalization of ¥12 million and borrowings of ¥25 million.

D. Kamiya

Trademark from July 1935 to April 1937

Trademark from April 1937 to present

Aug. 1937
Appointed Director and Manager of the Sales Department of the newly founded Toyota Motor Company, Ltd.

Truck Production in Japan, and Civilian/Military Demand: 1937-45

Year	Total production	Civilian use	Military use	Toyota production
1937	7,643	43.7	56.3	3,023
1938	13,981	74.7	25.3	3,719
1939	29,233	57.0	43.0	10,913
1940	42,093	48.9	51.1	13,574
1941	42,813	42.5	57.5	14,331
1942	34,786	44.4	55.6	16,261
1943	24,000	16.7	83.3	9,774
1944	21,434	16.1	83.9	12,701
1945	5,487	71.1	28.9	3,275

Source: "The 20-Year History of Toyota Motor Company."
Note: Units are vehicles and %.

1940

August 15, 1945 — End of War

At noon on August 15, 1945, the Japanese people heard the Emperor's broadcasted acceptance of the surrender terms of the Potsdam Declaration and realized that Japan had been defeated in war. In one instant the people were relieved of the fatigue and strain of a long war, but in the next instant they were overwhelmed with a feeling of despondency. The fear of food shortages, too, suddenly became very real.

Defeat in war marked the end of a period of militarism and the start of a period of democracy, and August 15 has been impressed in the memories of Japanese as a new starting point for the nation. Japanese also reflect back on August 15 when thinking about the path Japan will take in the future. Moreover, August 15 became a demarcation point in Japanese history that divides prewar and postwar days. A still finer distinction was made between generations: the prewar, wartime, and postwar generations.

Reconstruction Finance Bank

Japan experienced extremely severe inflation in the immediate postwar years. The major reason for this inflation was the Bank of Japan's issuance in January 1946 of additional bank notes worth ¥60 billion. To cope with the inflation, the government on February 26, 1946, enacted emergency financial measures, including the setting of price levels for rice and coal, and the setting of controls on the prices of other commodities. However, after enactment in October 1946 of the Reconstruction Finance Bank Act, inflation accelerated again. One cause of the new surge of inflation was the establishment of the Reconstruction Finance Bank. This Bank attempted to raise a large part of necessary government revenue through the issuing of public bonds, which led to the issuance of bonds without adequate backing and the issuing of a greater volume of new Bank of Japan notes.

Amidst such circumstances, Prime Minister Yoshida in December 1946 adopted a policy which put industries in priority categories. Those industries important for the nation's economic recovery were given top priority for receiving financial assistance from the government, and financial assistance to less critical industries was cut sharply. The coal industry had top priority, followed by the electric power, steel, fertilizer and shipping industries.

C. Toyota

Toyota's Motor Vehicle Production: 1935-45   Unit: vehicles

Year	Total production	Passenger cars	Trucks	Buses
1935	20	—	20	—
1936	1,142	100	910	132
1937	4,013	577	3,023	413
1938	4,615	539	3,719	357
1939	11,981	107	10,913	961
1940	14,787	268	13,574	945
1941	14,611	208	14,331	72
1942	16,302	41	16,261	—
1943	9,827	53	9,774	—
1944	12,720	19	12,701	—
1945	3,275	—	3,275	—

**Establishment of a Franchise System
— Preparing a Sales Network**

The franchise system of sales was first introduced
into Japan's automobile industry by Ford-Japan
and GM-Japan. Toyota began using the system
from when the company was established. Franchise systems were abolished during the war,
however, and a special company (the Jihai) was
established for distributing motor vehicles throughout the country. After the war, Kamiya worked
through Major Bunting and other persons to win
reestablishment of franchise systems in the automobile industry, and at the same time moved to
reorganize Toyota's sales network. The Jihai was
dissolved in June 1946 and franchise systems were
reintroduced. Toyota had begun preparing early
for this development and therefore succeeded in
building a sales network in the postwar period that
was even more powerful than its prewar network.

Jul. 1942
Temporary duty as Manag-
ing Director and Manager
of the Vehicle Department
of the Japan Motorcar Distribution System (Nippai).

111

Feb. 1946
Returned to Toyota Motor
Company as Director.

Size of Japan's War Losses in Various Categories	Unit: %
Value of national wealth	25.4
Buildings, structures	24.6
Ports, harbors, canals	7.5
Bridges	3.5
Industrial-use equipment and machinery	34.3
Railway lines	7.0
Vehicles	21.9
Ships, boats	80.6
Electric & gas supply facilities	10.8
Telephone, telegraph and broadcasting facilities	14.8
Waterworks	16.8
Owned assets	21.6
Miscellaneous	20.0
Difficult to classify	100.0

Source: Economic Planning Agency, Postwar History Editing Section,
"Postwar Economic History," 1957, p. 11.

GHQ Directive Concerning Restricted Concerns

One aspect of GHQ's administrative policies was the democratization of the Japanese economy. To do this it moved to convert Japanese industry to a peacetime orientation and to dissolve the zaibatsu. As a result, Mitsui and fourteen other zaibatsu received orders to freeze their assets. And to ensure the dissolution of the zaibatsu a Holding Company Liquidation Commission was established to which by the end of September 1947 the shareholdings of 83 holding companies were transferred. In addition, 4,500 companies, including subsidiaries and affiliates of the holding companies, were designated by the Commission as "restricted concerns." Toyota Motor Company was one of them. Restricted concerns were forbidden to own stock in another company or to have their personnel serve as staff members or employees of another company. Moreover, staff personnel or employees of a restricted concern were either forbidden to own any stock in another company or the number they could own was limited. These restrictions became a primary reason for the complete managerial independence of Toyota Motor Sales Company when it was established apart from Toyota Motor Company in June 1950.

Dodge Line

The "Dodge Line" refers to the economic measures proposed by Joseph Dodge in 1949 in order to fight inflation and let Japan gain its economic independence quickly. Dodge was president of the Detroit Bank and was in Japan as senior economic adviser to General MacArthur.

Among other measures, Dodge proposed a balanced budget and price differential subsidies. The subsidies went to companies that supplied products at official prices but suffered losses because of rising material costs. American foreign aid to Japan was also reduced, and Japan was forced to overcome its postwar inflation without help. These economic measures succeeded in stabilizing prices, but industry suffered greatly. Bankruptcies increased and unemployment rose. In 1952, the government finally turned away from the Dodge Line and began spending public funds to stimulate business.

C. Toyota

Passenger Car Production Begins Again

Toyota restarted its studies of passenger car production right after the war ended, and in 1947 it produced the Model SA, a small-size passenger car seating four persons. The Model SA was really an ambitious undertaking, and its construction was unique in that it employed a four-wheel independent suspension system. However, a number of external factors were against it. For example, SCAP's restriction on the production of passenger cars was in force until 1949, and only 300 passenger cars of 1500cc or less and 50 large-size cars could be produced annually. Moreover, no market yet existed for producing a passenger car in volume. Between 1947 and 1952 only 215 units of the Model SA passenger car were sold before it was discontinued.

D. Kamiya

Dec. 1946
Appointed Managing Director of Toyota Motor Company.

Apr. 1949
Appointed Director in the newly established Association for the Promotion of Automobile Exports. (Held this position until May 1966.)

1950

"The Postwar Period Is Already Over . . ."

In its Economic White Paper for 1955 the government wrote that economic recovery had been achieved and that high-growth was now being realized. "The postwar period is already over," government analysts commented. This phrase immediately became popular and was used widely outside the economics field when talking about new social fads and changes in the way people viewed their lives. The word "postwar" had been engraved deeply into the hearts of all Japanese as a reminder of their first defeat ever in war, and any consideration of Japanese society until 1955 had been made in a "postwar" context. The phrase in the Economic White Paper for 1955 had a powerful social impact, therefore, and it took on a significance much more important than being merely catchy wording.

Consumer Price Index, and
Rise in Mining & Industrial
Production: 1955-62

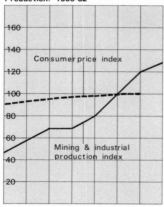

1955   56   57   58   59   60   61   62
Sources: Statistics of Japan, 1963, p.208;
         Economic White Paper, 1962, p.380.
Note: For Tokyo, with 1960 average as 100.

Sep. 1951
Japan signs peace treaties with forty-nine nations

Succession of Foreign Technical Tie-ups

In March 1952 MITI made clear its new position regarding the protection and nurturing of the domestic automobile industry. It emphasized the great influence of the industry on the national economy and the ripple effect of automobile technology on operations in other industries. As part of its moves to help Japanese automakers overcome their technological backwardness, MITI proposed that they import foreign technology or complete technical tie-ups with foreign companies.

Japanese automakers thus began actively negotiating with foreign automakers to complete technical agreements. Over ten different sets of negotiations actually took place, but the government authorized only four tie-ups: between Nissan and Austin (U.K.) in December 1952; between Hino Diesel and Renault (France) in March 1953; between Isuzu and Rootes (U.K.) also in March 1953; and between Mitsubishi and Willy's Overland (U.S.) in September 1953.

In order to understand this flurry of interest in foreign technical tie-ups it is important to realize the great concern in Japan at the time about the introduction of foreign capital into the automobile industry. Foreign automakers viewed the export of technology as an opportunity to establish a foothold in the Japanese market, and Japanese companies not then in the automobile industry viewed the import of foreign technology as an opportunity to prepare themselves quickly for entering the industry in the near future.

**Toyota's One and Only Labor Dispute,
Wide-Scale Social Repercussions**

Resigned as Managing Di-
rector of Toyota Motor
Company, and appointed
President of the newly
established Toyota Motor
Sales Company, Ltd.

The poor business conditions that followed the
retrenchment policies of the Dodge Line eventually
forced Toyota to revise its annual production plans
sharply downward from 15,840 to 3,000 vehicles,
and Toyota subsequently came to face its most
serious managerial crisis ever.

To reconstruct Toyota, a bank consortium formulated a plan that included the establishment of
Toyota Motor Sales Company and the layoff of a
large number of employees. On April 22, 1950,
Toyota called for volunteer resignations from
1,600 employees, but the labor union did not
accept the Company's plan, and a labor dispute
erupted. Thirty-six negotiation sessions between
labor and management were held from April 11th
to July 17th. Because of the labor dispute, production dropped from 992 vehicles in March, to
619 vehicles in April, to 304 vehicles in May.

On June 5, 1950, Toyota's management accepted
responsibility for the situation and resigned.
Agreement was then reached with labor on June 9,
and in July the production schedule returned to
normal.

Establishment of Toyota Motor Sales Company

Toyota Motor Sales Company was established on
April 3, 1950, with three main business objectives:
1) marketing automobiles and automobile
   components;
2) acting as an accident insurance agent;
3) performing all business related to the fore-
   going two items.

To carry out its business objectives, Toyota Motor
Sales adopted five basic policies. First, it would
operate from a completely autonomous position
without favoring either Toyota Motor Company or
Toyota dealers. Second, it would keep its profit
margin at the approximate level as Toyota's former
Sales Department, and therefore not cause an
increase in production costs. Third, it would strive
to raise its earnings power in order to foster its
own growth. Fourth, it would try to maintain a
close relationship with dealers and promote the
principle of coexistence and coprosperity with
them. Fifth, it would study new marketing
methods other than installment plans and insurance plans in order to develop the latent demand
for automobiles.

A. Socio-economic Background

Period of High Economic Growth

During 1955-56 Japan enjoyed the most favorable business conditions in its history, a culmination of the path from total war destruction, through reconstruction, into prosperity. A recession followed the favorable business period but it was short-lived and the government immediately turned again to direct policies promoting high economic growth.

The Economic White Paper of 1960 said that "technological innovations" and a "consumer revolution" had supplied the motivating force for high economic growth. It made two main points. First, that "investments called forth more investments," meaning that rapidly increased private investments in plants and facilities (¥1,370 billion in 1956, double the investments in 1955; ¥2,000 billion in 1959; over ¥3,000 billion in 1960; and over ¥4,000 billion in 1961) in order to raise productivity led to further investments in related industries. Second, that demands increased for new products that came from technological innovations, especially new consumer durables, which in turn stimulated private industry into making investments in equipment.

The government's "double incomes" plan announced in 1960 (government would aim to double workers' incomes during the period 1961-70) had a particularly strong effect not only on corporate activities but also on consumer behavior and the consumer consciousness. Out of this came moves to revolutionize the daily lives of the populace, beginning with "electrification" of home living. Products that emerged strongly around this time were home appliances, artificial fibers, automobiles, synthetic resins, and electronic goods. In connection with these products, investments were heavy in the steel, machinery, electric power and petroleum industries. The period of high economic growth in Japan coincided with a switch in energy sources from coal to oil and a switch to emphasis on the heavy and petrochemical industries.

B. Automobile Industry

First Japan Motor Show

The first Japan Motor Show, held in Tokyo's Hibiya Park for ten days beginning on April 20, 1954, attracted 540,000 viewers, thus demonstrating the strong interest that the general public had in automobiles. From 1959 the succeeding annual motor show was held at Harumi Pier in Tokyo, and from 1964 its name was changed to the Tokyo Motor Show. Gradually, moreover, the motor show changed in nature from being simply an annual event staged by the automobile industry to being a large event looked forward to each year by the public and widely covered by the mass media. The Tokyo Motor Show has influenced the way that the general public views the automobile, and it has played an important role in stimulating motorization's progress in Japan.

C. Toyota

Monthly Installment Financing

The financial market was still chaotic around this time. Consumer financing was impossible, and even the establishment of finance companies was impossible. Thus, installment sales of automobiles was extremely difficult. In this situation, Toyota Motor Sales moved to find a source of funds and to establish a system that would support installment sales. With cooperation from financial institutions Toyota developed a system whereby car buyers could buy on credit by signing promissory notes backed with collateral. In return for these notes, financial institutions provided Toyota with financing.

Use of this system effectively resolved Toyota's fund-raising problems. It also helped to modernize the management of dealerships, for in order to protect Toyota's credits a need arose to understand exactly how well dealers were operating their businesses, and this need led to establishment of a set of unified accounting procedures. Moreover, customer credit checks took on greater significance, and automobile companies began to realize the necessity of maintaining an orderly sales market.

Spread of Automobile Insurance System

Together with developing installment sales and installment financing systems, Toyota also developed a new automobile insurance system. Originally, the new system was aimed only at insuring credit payments in cases where cars were stolen or involved in fires, in serious accidents, or made inoperable in other ways. After insurance companies also began promoting various types of automobile insurance, however, the system became widespread even apart from the specific reason of covering future credit payments. Spread of the automobile insurance system helped the entire motorization process in Japan to move forward more smoothly.

Establishment of Tokyo Toyopet and Its Impact on Tokyo Market

Toyota established its first directly managed dealership in 1953. Called Tokyo Toyopet, this new dealership was capitalized at ¥30 million, of which 80 per cent was provided by Toyota and 20 per cent by existing dealerships. Toyota established the new dealership because it believed that securing an advantageous position in the Tokyo market, which then accounted for almost a third of the entire domestic automobile market, was essential for successful sales competition. Tokyo Toyopet subsequently contributed greatly to increasing Toyota's share of the Tokyo market. Whereas in 1952 Toyota's share of the Tokyo market was only 32.4 per cent (compared with 39.9 per cent of the nationwide market), by 1956 its share of that market had risen to 39.6 per cent (compared with 38.4 per cent of the nationwide market).

D. Kamiya

Mar. 1953
Appointed Chairman of the newly established Tokyo Toyopet Company. (Later appointed President.)

A. Socio-economic Background

Investments in Automobile,
Electric Machinery and
Petrochemical Industries:
1955-64

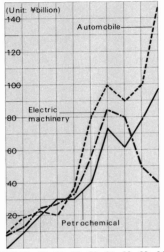

1955 56 57 58 59 60 61 62 63 64
Source: Economic Planning Agency,
Investment Plans of Major
Industries, 1965, pp. 200-09.

Feb. 1953
First public television broadcast
in Japan ushers in television age

B. Automobile Industry

Concept of "People's Car"

The Ministry of International
Trade and Industry (MITI) announced the following guidelines
for production of a "people's"
car, thus clarifying its willingness
to aid in the development of an
automobile with highly practical
features for use by the general
populace.

- Maximum speed of 100 kph or
  more, and fuel efficiency of 30
  km/l or more.
- Two to four passengers, and
  baggage capacity of 100kg or
  more.
- Engine displacement of 350-500
  cc.
- A production target of 2,000
  vehicles per month, and a unit
  production cost of 150,000 yen
  or less (later revised to a retail
  selling price of 250,000 yen or
  less).
- Production of prototypes by
  each automaker, within a schedule set by MITI, that meet the
  above specifications.
- MITI will conduct tests on the
  prototypes and will select the
  model most appropriate for
  mass production.
- MITI will earmark funds for improving and perfecting only the
  one model it selects.

Although the automobile industry
did not show great interest in
MITI's proposal, the proposal did
have a generally strong impact on
the public. It impressed the general populace with the fact that
an age of private-car use was fast
approaching.

Toyota had already begun planning and development of a mini-
car whose prototype, together
with discussions about a "people's" car, became a subject of
wide interest. This mini-car was
the Publica, Model UP10,
Toyota's entry to the popular car
market.

C. Toyota

College Graduates Employed as Salesmen

Toyota in 1953 employed about 100 new college graduates and trained them as salesmen in its directly managed Tokyo Toyopet Company. Companies had not previously used college graduates as house salesmen, but Toyota believed that upgrading the image of salesmen was necessary in order to impress on the public the fact that the automobile is a sophisticated product. Toyota also believed that if motorization was to spread in Japan, it was absolutely necessary first to raise the social status of automobile salesmen. Toyota's move was copied in other industries later, and the social status of salesmen did indeed rise.

Introduction of SKB Light Truck

Toyota introduced the Model SKB light truck in January 1954 in hopes of penetrating the large market for three-wheel trucks. The SKB truck is significant in Toyota's history because it was Toyota's first vehicle developed through product planning based on definite marketing goals, and because its development was a major factor prompting Toyota to switch to a multiple dealership system. Renamed the Toyo-Ace in 1956 after a public contest, the SKB truck sold well and gained a large share of the three-wheel truck market. Its sales were boosted particularly by Toyota's progressive pricing policy and by the fact that Toyota introduced a new marketing channel for the vehicle — the Toyopet Dealers, established in 1956-57.

The success of the Toyo-Ace truck had a great impact on the Japanese automobile industry. Besides the previous bonnet-type truck designed for carrying both freight and passengers, all domestic manufacturers now began producing cab-over type trucks designed especially for carrying freight. Moreover, the resulting creation of a market for cab-over trucks led to a rapid decline in demand for three-wheel trucks. The Toyo-Ace was thus not only a best-seller for Toyota, but also a revolutionary new force in the automobile market, ushering in a new age in commercial vehicle production.

Chubu Nippon Driving School

Toyota realized fully that in order to promote the spread of motorization it was first necessary to increase the number of people having driver's licenses. In 1957, therefore, Toyota opened the Chubu Nippon Driving School, the largest of its kind in Asia. The fact that a company capitalized at ¥1 billion would invest ¥400 million in a driving school was called "reckless" by some people. But this school contributed greatly to the spread of motorization in Japan by being a first step in the long-term development of automobile demand.

D. Kamiya

A. Socio-economic Background

B. Automobile Industry

Demand for Passenger Cars in Taxi and For-hire Industry

During the period when the full benefits of mass production were still not being realized in the automobile industry in Japan, and when the demand in the private sector for passenger cars was small, taxi and for-hire companies accounted for 70 per cent of the entire passenger car market. But the competition with imports for this market was intense, and Japanese automakers had to produce vehicles with specifications that met the needs of the taxi and for-hire companies. The first difficulty was development of technology needed to build sturdy vehicles.

Sharp Rise in Individual Demand for Motor Vehicles

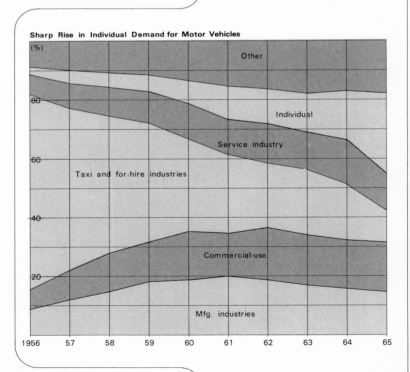

Number of Certified Driving Schools and Number of Licensed Drivers: 1961-69

Year	No. of schools	No. of licensed drivers	% of total pop.
1961	125	11,939	12.7
1962	316	13,920	14.6
1963	520	16,212	16.9
1964	764	18,990	19.5
1965	981	21,104	21.2
1966	1,085	22,857	23.3
1967	1,153	24,697	24.9
1968	1,185	26,343	26.3
1969	1,235	24,513	23.5

Notes: In addition to certified schools, in July 1969 there were 479 uncertified schools;
unit for number of drivers is thousand persons; figures on licensed drivers are
for end October each year; in 1969 revisions were made in method of computing
data for number of licensed drivers.
Source: National Police Agency

Expansion and Improvement of Toyota's After-sales Service Organization

From its inception, Toyota emphasized after-sales service and made various efforts to improve its after-sales service organization. As early as 1937 it started a program of technical training for dealer mechanics.

The rapid spread of motorization in the postwar period led to a shortage of trained servicemen, and to cope with this shortage Toyota in 1961 established the Chubu Automobile Maintenance School, Japan's first institution for training automobile mechanics.

Another step taken by Toyota to strengthen the Company's after-sales service organization was the establishment of Toyopet Maintenance Company. This company repairs vehicles which cannot be repaired by dealers and builds to order special prototype vehicles. It also carries out mandatory two-year inspections and complete overhauls on trade-ins.

Introduction of Crown and Corona Models

The Toyopet Crown RS, marketed by Toyota in January 1955, represented a total mobilization of Toyota's resources, and in many ways the Company's future depended on the new model's success in the marketplace. Previously all domestically manufactured passenger cars featured a truck chassis, but the Crown was developed with special attention given to the design of a pure passenger car in all structural aspects, including the chassis. Consequently, the Crown featured many technological innovations.

A. Socio-economic Background	B. Automobile Industry

A. Socio-economic Background

May 1955
Brisk sales of washing machines, juice mixers, electric cookers and other electric home appliances usher in home "electrification" age

Oct. 1956
Japan-U.S.S.R. resume diplomatic relations

Dec. 1956
Japan admitted to United Nations

C. Toyota

Introduction of the Crown had a great impact on the Japanese automobile industry. Until then there was much controversy in Japan about the relative merits of foreign and domestic vehicles, and even some experts involved in fostering development of the domestic automobile industry did not highly evaluate the technological competence of domestic manufacturers. The Crown, however, provided decisive support for protection of the domestic auto industry, demonstrating conclusively that Japanese manufacturers were capable of improving their technological capabilities. Moreover, the Crown helped establish clear goals in government administration of Japan's automobile industry. The Crown thus was extremely important in Toyota's history. It not only made a success out of Toyota's "gamble" to establish passenger car assembly in Japan using only domestic technology, but it also contributed greatly to heightening Toyota's corporate image and public reputation.

After introduction of the Crown, Toyota next introduced the Toyopet Corona ST10 in 1957 as a step in penetrating the small-vehicle market then expanding because of strong demand for taxis. This vehicle featured a monocoque body, a new type of front suspension developed independently by Toyota, and a new axle design unique among domestic passenger cars at the time.

First Crown model (1955).

First Corona model (1957).

D. Kamiya

Sep. 1956
Appointed Adviser to the Ministry of Trade and Industry. (Held this position until August 1957.)

Feb. 1957
Appointed Director of the Okagakuen School in Nagoya.

A. Socio-economic Background

B. Automobile Industry

New Models in Toyota Line

	Models Handled
"Toyota" Dealers	Century, Crown, Carina, Carina Van
"Toyopet" Dealers	Corona Mark II, Corona Mark II Van, Corona, Corona Van, Toyo-Ace, Hi-Ace
"Dieasel" Dealers	Dyna, Stout, Hi-Lux Land Cruiser, Large-size trucks, ambulances
"Corolla" Dealers	Celica, Corolla, Corolla Van
"Auto" Dealers	Sprinter, Starlet, Publica, Publica Van, Publica Pick-up, Lite-Ace
Totals	

C. Toyota

Multiple Marketing Channels

The traditional automobile marketing system of one dealer per prefecture was replaced by a system of multiple marketing channels. This move strengthened Toyota's over-all marketing capabilities and became an important factor later in promoting the policy of dividing the market by vehicle model. The success of the multiple marketing channels system enabled Toyota to secure and maintain a high share in each segment of the market, and enabled it to introduce the sales strategy of developing new products, establishing new marketing channels for the new products, and thus creating a new demand for automobiles.

Increased Number of Dealer Outlets

Number of Outlets by Year

1950	51	52	53	54	55	56	57	58	59	60	61	62	63	64	65	66	67	67	69	70
47	47	47	49	49	49	49	49	49	49	49	49	49	49	49	49	49	49	49	49	49
			1	1	1	40	51	51	51	51	51	51	53	53	53	53	53	52	52	52
							7	9	9	9	9	9	9	9	11	11	11	11	6	4
											31	56	63	65	69	86	85	80	83	84
																	3	45	61	62
47	47	47	50	50	50	89	107	109	109	109	140	165	174	176	182	199	201	237	251	251

A. Socio-economic Background

B. Automobile Industry

Toyota's Exports to the United States: 1956-63   Unit: vehicles

Year	Total exports	Pass cars	% of total
1956	6	0	0
1957	10	8	80.0
1958	741	703	94.9
1959	1,429	1,171	81.9
1960	507	316	62.3
1961	407	87	21.4
1962	1,093	91	8.3
1963	1,164	17	1.5

Source: Toyota Motor Sales Co., Ltd.

126

C. Toyota

First Japanese Automaker to Export to U.S.

Toyota had long dreamed of exporting a domestic-made passenger car to the American market. And although many people called Toyota reckless at the time, the Company in 1957 exported its first passenger cars to the United States. Toyota at one time was forced to pull out of the American market temporarily, but its early experience there afterward stimulated its engineers into developing products capable of meeting international standards of quality. The first two of these products were the new Corona and the Corolla.

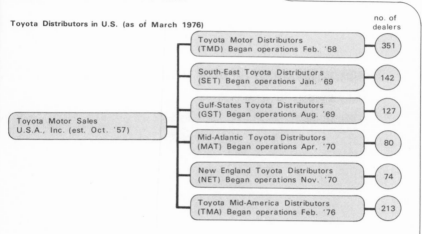

Toyota Distributors in U.S. (as of March 1976)

	no. of dealers
Toyota Motor Distributors (TMD) Began operations Feb. '58	351
South-East Toyota Distributors (SET) Began operations Jan. '69	142
Gulf-States Toyota Distributors (GST) Began operations Aug. '69	127
Mid-Atlantic Toyota Distributors (MAT) Began operations Apr. '70	80
New England Toyota Distributors (NET) Began operations Nov. '70	74
Toyota Mid-America Distributors (TMA) Began operations Feb. '76	213

Toyota Motor Sales U.S.A., Inc. (est. Oct. '57)

Sales Training Organization

Based on the conviction that the nation-wide training of salesmen was the quickest and most effective way of modernizing its sales organization, Toyota Motor Sales Company in 1956 initiated a program for training salesmen to become sales managers. This first program depended on outside instructors, but Toyota later moved to design a permanent sales training program and to educate its own personnel to be instructors. In 1958, the Company established the Toyota Sales College — the first such school in the indstury — inside the Chubu Nippon Automobile School. Toyota bolstered the Sales College's training staff as the number of trainees increased, and to round out the program later introduced a special course for managers.

Dealers eventually asked that Toyota design special on-site seminars to train their new employees as well as sub-dealer personnel. The activities of the Toyota Sales College thus expanded, and Toyota came to have a sales training organization in operation even before automobiles began to sell in volume in Japan. In that sense, Toyota was a step ahead of other automakers in improving the quality of its salesmen, a point which took on great significance in later marketing strategies.

D. Kamiya

127

A. Socio-economic Background

B. Automobile Industry

128

Honsha Plant (1938).

Motomachi Plant (1959).

C. Toyota

Toward Production of 30,000 Vehicles Monthly

In 1959 Toyota began moving forcefully to put its facilities into order for mass production of passenger cars. That year it completed its first-stage construction of its Motomachi Plant, which tied to introduction of the Publica in 1961. Partsmakers also made equipment investments. They built new plants and installed automatic machinery, and succeeded in reducing the unit cost of parts.

Toyota's production system was thus fairly well organized by early 1963 when business conditions began to improve. Its plants started operating at full capacity: in March 1963, Toyota's monthly production exceeded 25,000 units; in May, 27,000 units; and in October Toyota reached its long-awaited production target of 30,000 vehicles a month. In June 1963, just three years and five months after being marketed, the Publica series set a cumulative production record of over 200,000 units.

Trends Since 1955 in Toyota's Investments
in Plants and Facilities

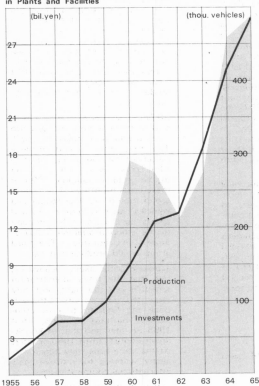

D. Kamiya

Jul. 1959
Appointed Managing Director of the Chiyoda Fire & Marine Insurance Co., Ltd.

1960

A. Socio-economic Background

Liberalization of Trade and Capital

In January 1960 the Japanese government established a Council for Promoting the Liberalization of Trade, and began taking active steps for liberalizing imports. Thereafter, the percentage of liberalized items among total imports rose steadily. These items accounted for 62 per cent of the total value of imports in April 1961, 88 per cent in October 1962 and 93 per cent in October 1964. In October 1965, moreover, the import of automobiles was liberalized, marking just about the complete opening of Japan to world trade. Meanwhile, another demand — the liberalization of capital movements — was being made on Japan by the OECD member states, especially after April 1964 when Japan joined the OECD. In July 1967, the Japanese government implemented its first set of capital liberalization measures, and followed them with a second set in March 1969 and a third set in September 1970. In June 1971 additional liberalization was introduced in six auto-related industries, permitting up to 50 per cent participation. In August 1971 the government implemented a fourth set of measures, and finally, in May 1973, it implemented its fifth set, thus introducing 100 per cent capital liberalization, with very few exceptions.

In these circumstances, talk grew lively about the need to reorganize industry in order to strengthen the international competitiveness of Japanese companies. Even as such discussion progressed, large corporations began merging. Perhaps the best-known is the merger in 1970 of Yawata Iron and Steel Works and Fuji Iron and Steel Works to form Nippon Steel Corporation.

Apr. 1960
Japan accepted into IMF with Article 8 status

Apr. 1960
Japan accepted as member state in OECD

130

B. Automobile Industry

MITI Concept of Three Company Groups for Producing Passenger Cars

In May 1961 MITI announced that imports of completely built-up passenger cars would be liberalized in the spring of 1963 (actually liberalized in 1965), and revealed a plan it had formulated for strengthening the international competitiveness of Japan's automobile industry in order to meet the challenges of liberalization.

MITI planned first of all to exclude imports of passenger cars and engine components from the immediate liberalization schedule because domestic passenger cars were still not competitive and because engine components were essential in order for foreign automakers to enter the Japanese market via knock-down assembly operations. But MITI knew it would be difficult to postpone complete liberalization indefinitely and stressed that Japanese automakers should bolster their competitiveness. One step MITI took was direct administrative guidance to help automakers reduce costs.

MITI's plan called for grouping two or three companies each into three production groups by 1963. The first group would produce passenger cars on a mass production basis, with each company in the group producing 7,000 or more units monthly. The second group would produce specialized vehicles, such as luxury cars and sports cars, with each company in the group producing 3,000 or more units monthly. The third group would produce mini-cars.

Japanese automakers, meanwhile, felt that the trade liberalization schedule was too tight, and they requested the government to postpone the liberalization of completely built-up imports until 1965 or later and that of knock-down imports until 1968 or later. At the same time they began earnestly working to improve their international competitiveness.

Although the domestic passenger car market had begun expanding rapidly, however, market shares

Development of Popular Car Market

Toyota's Publica was the first car in Japan marketed specifically for the mass market. Although the system of Publica dealers was modeled along the lines of the American system of multiple dealers, conditions peculiar to the Japanese market prevented effective use of the main features of that system, i.e., small-scale dealers, open territories and wholesale cash-on-delivery.

The open territory system fit the American situation because dealers there depended mainly on showroom visitors for sales, but in Japan the traditional way of selling cars is to make house calls. Also, small-scale dealers had trouble raising funds, and the cash-on-delivery system had to be replaced with a system of sales based on wholesale promissory notes.

Because of these difficulties Toyota revised its original sales targets (3,000 vehicles/month to begin with and 10,000 vehicles/month in the near-term future) and opened a large, directly managed dealership in Tokyo in January 1962.

While Toyota's revised sales organization was a retreat from its original plans, the new sales network later served Toyota well when popular-size cars began selling in great numbers.

Reinforcing Export Organization

In 1962 Toyota Motor Sales Company established an Export Headquarters with four departments in charge of separate export zones. These departments follow their markets closely and make detailed recommendations that are reflected in export policy. Also, an Export Administration Department was established in order to coordinate the activities of all the departments in Export Headquarters and to conduct over-all export planning. These changes bolstered Toyota's export activities in administrative and personnel terms. In September 1959 there were 52 employees engaged in export activities. This figure dropped a year later to 46, but rose again in 1961 to 58. With establishment of Export Headquarters on February 1, 1962, the figure rose to 150, and in September 1962 it was 221. Toyota later opened a Technical Department in Export Headquarters in order to meet the growing need for overseas technical guidance brought on by an increase in the number of knock-down vehicles it was exporting.

May 1960
Awarded Order of the Blue Ribbon for meritorious service.

May 1960
Appointed Acting Director of the Tokai Bank.

Sep. 1961
Appointed President of the newly established Chukyo Television Broadcasting Company. (Renamed the Nagoya Broadcasting Company in December 1961.)

May 1962
Awarded Order of the Dark-blue Ribbon for meritorious service.

A. Socio-economic Background

Structural Recession

In its Economic White Paper for 1965, the government referred to the recession of 1965 as being "structural" in nature rather than being caused by environmental factors. Subsequently the expression "structural" recession came into vogue, although it is not a common economic term. Recessions usually had their origins in stagnation of the business environment that accompanied a need to adjust inventories, but the recession of 1965 occurred as changes were being made in the industrial structure and in structural aspects of the economic environment. The economy could not recover on its own, and the recession became prolonged. This same recession is sometimes called a "policy" recession, because some people felt that the government either made wrong economic decisions or made no decisions at all, thus bringing on a recession but doing nothing about it.

Oct. 1964
New Tokaido "bullet" Line opens between Tokyo and Osaka

Oct. 1964
Tokyo Olympics

July 1965
Meishin Expressway completed between Nagoya and Kobe, marking Japan's entrance into true highway period

B. Automobile Industry

were not distributed evenly and MITI's plan for reorganizing the industry had the negative effect of increasing the competition among companies to such an extent that its original aims could not be entirely met. Despite the failings of MITI's plan, it has historical significance because it stimulated serious discussions about restructuring the Japanese automobile industry.

Japan-U.S. Automobile Negotiations

From December 1967, at the request of the government of the United States, a Japanese-U.S. Conference was held in Tokyo to discuss the liberalization of automobile imports into Japan. The American side emphasized five main items.

1. The import duties set on motor vehicles as a result of negotiations at the Kennedy Round are 3 per cent for the United States and 17.5 per cent for Japan. This difference is still much too great.
2. The system of commodity taxes in Japan is disadvantageous to American-made motor vehicles and should be revised. In particular, the high tax rate on large-size passenger cars should be lowered.
3. The road tax on large-size passenger cars in Japan is unfairly high.
4. The import allocation system concerning engines and other important motor vehicle components is biased and should be corrected.
5. The liberalization of capital in the automobile industry should be according to the same schedule in Japan as in the United States.

Neither party gave way, but the United States continued to press for acceptance of its demands and asked especially for a clear schedule for liberalizing engine imports, a precondition to entry into Japan for knock-down operations. The Japanese government felt that any further worsening of Japan-U.S. relations might negatively influence business in other industries exporting to the United

C. Toyota

New Corona and Corolla: Success in Mass Production

In September 1964 Toyota marketed the Model RT-40 Corona passenger car. This car was the result of all-out efforts by Toyota to develop a passenger car that would meet the requirements of the highway age that was just starting in Japan while also meeting the challenges of trade liberalization.

Toyota had paid particular consideration to making the new Corona a car fitting for export markets, and from the planning stages it emphasized high-level performance and quality standards. In effect, the new Corona was designed as "a car fitting for use on American highways." Once on sale, its superior performance capabilities and advanced design, combined with bold production and marketing policies, made it an immediate success. In fact, it was the best-selling car in Japan for thirty-three consecutive months beginning in April 1965. It rewrote the entire record book for Japanese-made cars in production, sales and export. In 1969, moreover, it was ranked fifth among the top production models in the world, with 430,000 vehicles produced for the year.
After the new Corona, Toyota in November 1966 marketed the Corolla, a smaller car than the Corona. Japan's automobile market had begun to expand, and the Corolla — backed by superior styling and performance characteristics, and tremendous advance publicity — took the lead in the small-car market from the day it went on sale. In May 1967 the Corolla series was produced for the first time at a rate of 10,000 vehicles a month; in June 1976 the Corolla passenger car model alone was produced at that rate.

Not long after marketing the Corolla domestically, Toyota also introduced it to the export market as a "family car for the world." The Corolla thus took its place with the Crown and Corona models as a passenger car fitting for overseas markets.

The Sprinter was added to the top of the Corolla series in May 1968, and sales in December 1968 of the entire series — including the Corolla van — were 29,500 vehicles; an additional 4,500 vehicles were exported during that month. Sales of the Corolla continued to be brisk at home and abroad, and in February 1969 cumulative production of the model reached 500,000 vehicles. One year later — only 42 months after the Corolla was marketed — its cumulative production passed the million mark. The Corolla was the first Japanse-made car to reach the million production figure in such a short time, which put it in a production class with passenger cars like Ford's Mustang and others.

D. Kamiya

Oct. 1962
Appointed Director of the Japan Automobile Federation.

Jul. 1963
Appointed Auditor of Toyota Motor Company, Ltd.

Nov. 1963
Appointed Standing Member of the Nagoya Chamber of Commerce.

May 1964
Appointed Auditor of the Chiyoda Mutual Life Insurance Company.

A. Socio-economic Background

Revaluation of Yen

Japan accumulated large holdings of foreign currency reserves starting in 1965, and in 1970 — despite poor business conditions — the reserves totalled $5.5 billion. In the United States, meanwhile, the inflation rate rose and the trade balance worsened steadily from 1966. As a result, worldwide confidence in the dollar dropped. Beginning around 1967, moreover, when U.S. gold reserves fell below the country's external dollar liabilities, confidence in the dollar fell decisively. On August 15, 1971, President Nixon temporarily suspended all exchange of dollars to gold, and announced a set of economic measures to protect the dollar, including a 10 per cent surcharge on imports. Nixon's announcement caused Japan's stock markets to plunge, and set off massive selling of dollars. On August 28 the government was forced to float the yen. The Bank of Japan intervened to keep the exchange rate somewhat stable, but its action brought strong domestic and overseas protests. In response to Japanese requests, the United States finally dropped the surcharge on imports on the condition that Japan agree to revalue the yen upward. Then, on December 20, 1971, at a meeting of economic ministers held at the Smithsonian Institute in Washington, a new monetary agreement was reached, and Japan's currency was revalued from ¥360 to ¥308 to the dollar.

July 1969
Tomei Expressway opens between Tokyo and Nagoya

B. Automobile Industry

States, and in August 1968 indicated that by early 1972 it would liberalize the import of engines.

While it seemed that a settlement was thus reached in these eight-month-long negotiatons, the two problems of capital liberalization and of the conditions acceptable for tie-ups between American and Japanese automakers surfaced in 1969, and various demands once more came from the United States. In Japan, arguments on the pros and cons of capital liberalization grew intense not only in the automobile industry but also in government and in business circles.

Lively Discussions About Capital Liberalization

Automobile talks between Japan and the United States ended in August 1968 without touching on a clear time schedule for the liberalization of capital in the Japanese automobile industry, a point which the American side had strongly wanted to clarify, or on problems about the kind of tie-ups that the Japanese government would permit between American and Japanese companies. Early in 1969 the United States again began strongly requesting replies from the Japanese government on those two subjects.

Japanese automakers expected to complete the reorganizaton of the automobile industry by the end of 1971, and took the stand that the government should introduce capital liberalization in 1973 or later. After Mitsubishi announced its tie-up with Chrysler in May 1969, however, business circles began talking about early capital liberalization in the automobile industry. In this general context the government set October 1971 as the official date for capital liberalization, and the automobile industry thus had to prepare itself quickly for a completely open system of trade.

C. Toyota

World's Top Production Models (1969)

Rank	Model	Manufacturer	Country	Production for Year
1	Beetle	VW	W.Germany	1,081,203
2	Chevrolet	GM	U.S.	1,069,437
3	Ford	Ford	U.S.	876,196
4	Corona	Toyota	Japan	434,479
5	Buick	GM	U.S.	434,382
6	Chevelle	GM	U.S.	401,256
7	Oldsmobile	GM	U.S.	373,028
8	Pontiac	GM	U.S.	358,838
9	Fiat 500	Fiat	Italy	346,559
10	Corolla	Toyota	Japan	340,761
11	Bluebird	Nissan	Japan	337,486

Note: Commercial vehicles excluded.
Sources: Motor vehicle manufacturers associations in the respective countries.

Toyota's Business Ties with Hino Motors and Daihatsu Kogyo

Japan's automobile industry began reorganizing itself in the mid-1960s in order to meet the challenges of capital liberalization. The merger between Nissan and Prince in 1966, and the business tie completed between Mitsubishi and Chrysler in 1969 are two examples of this trend. Toyota, meanwhile, completed business ties with Hino Motors in 1966 and with Daihatsu Kogyo in 1967.

In production, Toyota entrusted Hino Motors with assembly of the Publica Van in order to utilize Hino's production facilities efficiently. In marketing, the companies coordinated their activities in various ways: Hino reorganized its sales network so that it centered on large-size cars, for example, and Toyota helped Hino with its small-car sales and its after-sales servicing. This policy worked quite well. The Toyota Briska (GY-10) truck, which Toyota marketed in April 1967 and developed from the Hino Briska, was one result of the tie-up with Hino. The Briska was an important product that helped Toyota to maintain its share of the one-ton bonnet truck market.

In its second tie-up, Toyota worked jointly with Daihatsu to develop new passenger car models, and in 1969 the two companies introduced two models with interchangeable parts, the Toyota Publica and the Daihatsu Consorte Berlina. Toyota also entrusted Daihatsu with production of the Publica Sedan, which, along with production of the Publica Hi-Lux truck by Hino Motors, promoted development of an over-all mass production system.

Feb. 1965
Appointed member of National Police Agency's Tokyo Municipal Traffic Safety Committee.

May 1966
Appointed Director of the newly established Automobile Manufacturers Association. (Resigned from the post in May 1974.)

Jun. 1967
Received Prime Minister's Award for achievements in promoting exports.

135

Moves to Restructure Automobile Industry

MITI's proposal to reorganize the automobile industry into three groups of companies stimulated discussions about reorganization as a means of strengthening the industry's international competitiveness in order to prepare for eventual, all-out trade liberalization. In fact, the discussions gradually spread to include the general restructuring of Japanese industry.

Reorganization occurred in two stages in the automobile industry: in 1965-67, before capital liberalization had emerged as a serious problem; and from 1969 onward, after the schedule for capital liberalization had become fairly clear.

The first stage of reorganization began with the signing in May 1965 of a merger agreement between Nissan and Prince (merger finalized in August 1966). Next, Toyota and Hino completed a business tie-up in October 1966,

Isuzu and Fuji Heavy Industries completed a tie-up in December 1966 (dissolved in May 1968), and Toyota and Daihatsu completed a tie-up in November 1967. Other tie-ups were completed even as Japan-U.S. automobile talks were being conducted in 1968. Isuzu and Mitsubishi completed a business tie-up in June (dissolved in May 1969 when Mitsubishi announced a tie-up with Chrysler) and Nissan and Fuji Heavy Industries completed a tie-up in October. That year marked the end of hectic moves in the first stage of the industry's reorganization.

In 1969, however, Mitsubishi's announcement of a business tie-up with Chrysler signalled a new wave of ties between companies. In March 1970 Nissan and Isuzu completed a tie-up, and in July 1971 Isuzu and GM completed a tie-up.

136

Takaoka Plant (1966).

C. Toyota

Annual Production of One Million, and Then Two Million Vehicles

Production of 1.47 million motor vehicles in 1969 moved Toyota ahead of Fiat into fifth position in the world after GM, Ford, VW and Chrysler. Thereafter, Toyota expanded and improved its production facilities and marketing network in order to establish and support a system for producing two million vehicles annually. That system would enable Toyota to meet the challenges at home related to the approaching liberalization of capital, and to become more active in world markets. After completion of its Kamigo Plant in November 1965, its Takaoka Plant in December 1966, and its Miyoshi Plant in July 1968, Toyota in July 1969 began construction of its Tsutsumi Plant, its sixth plant.

In its marketing network, Toyota had 180 dealers in Japan in 1965. The number increased to 222 in 1968 and to 251 by the end of 1969. Between the end of 1965 and the end of 1969, moreover, the number of dealer employees increased from 48,000 to 78,000; the number of dealer salesmen doubled from 10,000 to 20,000; and the number of dealer showrooms increased from 1,200 to 2,500.

Toyota also strengthened its export system around this time, stimulated especially by introduction of the new Corona and the Corolla. Exports eventually were to be shipped to 143 distributors in 140 countries.

As a result of improving its domestic and export systems, Toyota in 1972 reached the two million mark in annual production.

D. Kamiya

Nov. 1967
Appointed Auditor of the Toyoda Automatic Loom Works Company.

Nov. 1968
Received Second Order of Merit of the Rising Sun.

Jun. 1969
Appointed Chairman of the Chiyoda Fire & Marine Insurance Co., Ltd.

World's Top Automakers in Number of Vehicles Produced: 1969-72   Unit: vehicles

Rank	1969 Company	Production	1970 Company	Production	1971 Company	Production	1972 Company	Production
1	GM (U.S.)	5,255,370	GM	3,593,723	GM	5,764,386	GM	5,741,448
2	Ford (U.S.)	2,821,643	Ford	2,657,832	Ford	2,819,077	Ford	3,196,858
3	VW (W.Germany)	1,639,630	VW	1,621,197	Toyota	1,955,033	Toyota	2,087,133
4	Chrysler (U.S.)	1,557,659	Toyota	1,609,190	VW	1,715,905	Nissan	1,864,244
5	Toyota (Japan)	1,471,211	Fiat	1,523,452	Nissan	1,591,490	Chrysler	1,693,080
6	Fiat (Italy)	1,311,114	Chrysler	1,452,044	Chrysler	1,518,072	VW	1,477,343
7	Nissan (Japan)	1,148,715	Nissan	1,374,022	Fiat	1,461,836	Fiat	1,453,115
8	BLMC (U.K.)	1,016,280	Renault	1,159,745	Renault	1,174,314	Renault	1,318,327
9	Renault (France)	1,009,372	BLMC	961,705	BLMC	1,060,956	BLMC	1,140,000
10	Opel (W.Germany)	801,205	Opel	820,852	Opel	838,718	Opel	877,481

1970

Mar. 1970
Osaka World's Fair, EXPO '70, begins

Oct. 1970
National Census figures published: Japan's population 103,703,522 persons, surpassing 100 million for first time

Aug. 1971
U.S. President Nixon announces emergency economic measures to defend dollar; Japan's stock exchanges suffer sharpest drop in history

Sep. 1972
Japan-China resume diplomatic relations

Oct. 1973
OPEC oil blockade

Isuzu Motors Announces Tie-up with General Motors

Isuzu Motors announced in November 1970 that it would enter into a business tie-up with General Motors, an agreement which was formalized in July 1971 with C. Itoh & Company as the intermediary. The suddenness of the decision, and the fact that C. Itoh & Company was involved, caused much surprise in the industry. Together with this agreement, the existing business relationship between Isuzu Motors and Nissan Motor Company was dissolved.

Mitsubishi Heavy Industries Announces Tie-up with Chrysler Corporation

The Chrysler Corporation was the first of the U.S. Big Three automakers to enter into a business tie-up with a Japanese company. It made an agreement with Mitsubishi Heavy Industries in May 1969. In June 1970, Mitsubishi separated its automotive division to create Mitsubishi Motors.

Automobile Industry Grows Tremendously

The automobile industry, like the steel industry, is one of the main industries supporting Japan's economy. As a leading industry it has come to occupy an important economic position.

In 1974 the value of automobile manufacturing production was ¥9,183.4 billion, which was 8.4 per cent of the total value of manufacturing production that year. That figure, moreover, was only for companies directly involved in production, and the percentage rises much higher if related industries are included. Because of the size of the automobile's aftermarket, the automobile industry also plays an important role in creating job opportunities. The industry's influence on the lives of the populace is today a very great one.

C. Toyota

Toyota's Corolla Becomes World's Top Production Model

The Toyota Corolla was fourth among the world's top production models in 1973, behind Volkswagen's Beetle, GM's Chevrolet, and the Ford. In 1974, however, the Corolla became the world's top production model, and it held the number one position again in 1975, with production of 649,000 units.

Toyota Exported Its 5-millionth Vehicle in May 1975

Toyota's first exports were the shipment abroad of four trucks in 1936. Exports did not begin in earnest, however, until the latter half of the 1960s. They reached an annual total of 100,000 vehicles for the first time in 1966, and in 1969 the accumulated total number of exports passed the one million mark. In May 1975, Toyota exported its 5-millionth vehicle.

D. Kamiya

Mar. 1972
Appointed Chairman of the Toyota Technical Senior High School.

Jun. 1972
Received honorary doctor's degree in the humanities from the University of Utah in the United States.

Nov. 1973
Awarded First Order of Merit, and Order of the Sacred Treasure.

Dec. 1975
Appointed Chairman of Toyota Motor Sales Co., Ltd.

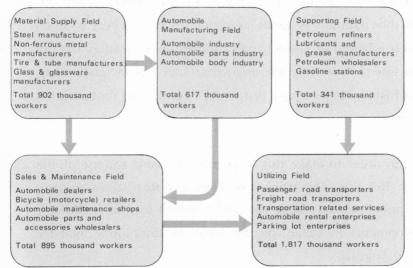

The automobile industry as a major industry

There are 15 million persons directly employed in the Japanese automobile industry.
If persons engaged in indirect work related to the industry are included,
this figure increases to 10% of the country's total labor force.

Material Supply Field

Steel manufacturers
Non-ferrous metal manufacturers
Tire & tube manufacturers
Glass & glassware manufacturers

Total 902 thousand workers

Automobile Manufacturing Field

Automobile industry
Automobile parts industry
Automobile body industry

Total 617 thousand workers

Supporting Field

Petroleum refiners
Lubricants and grease manufacturers
Petroleum wholesalers
Gasoline stations

Total 341 thousand workers

Sales & Maintenance Field

Automobile dealers
Bicycle (motorcycle) retailers
Automobile maintenance shops
Automobile parts and accessories wholesalers

Total 895 thousand workers

Utilizing Field

Passenger road transporters
Freight road transporters
Transportation related services
Automobile rental enterprises
Parking lot enterprises

Total 1,817 thousand workers

SOURCE: Number of workers based on Prime Minister's Office Statistics of Business Locations, 1972; and Ministry of International Trade and Industry, Trade in Japan, 1973.

POSTSCRIPT

The main text of *My Life With Toyota* is from a series of articles that I wrote for the *Nihon Keizai Shimbun* in late summer 1974. The articles are used here with the generous consent of that newspaper.

Generally, I do not like spending time on matters that have passed. One of life's lessons to me has been to let the past be, and to concentrate on what I will do tomorrow to improve myself. But the editors of the *Nihon Keizai Shimbun* asked me specifically for an account of my personal experiences, and this book thus naturally depends largely on my past. There is much reference herein to Toyota and to Japan's motorization, but my main intent in writing the original articles was to relate a personal history rather than a history of Toyota or of motorization in Japan.

Also, in order to make this book more readable and useful, the Public Relations Department of Toyota Motor Sales Company has appended to it background information on socio-economic developments in Japan, on the Japanese automobile industry and on Toyota.

The Asian Games uses the slogan "Ever Onward," and the Games urge the youth of Asia to be courageous in life as they face the challenges of their potential. The slogan is a good one, and young people everywhere, not only in Asia, certainly should accept life's challenges. Life to me has seemed to be an unending struggle with the limits of human possibility, and this book has forced me to reflect back on the road I have taken. My reflections have reinforced my belief that life is an unending struggle with one's own possibilities.

If the personal experiences I have related in this book contribute in any way toward a clearer appreciation of the development process of the Japanese automobile industry, I could feel no greater satisfaction.

Shotaro Kamiya
Chairman
Toyota Motor Sales Co., Ltd.